Six Jewish Spiritual Paths

Six Jewish Spiritual Paths

A RATIONALIST LOOKS

AT SPIRITUALITY

RABBI RIFAT SONSINO

For People of All Faiths, All Backgrounds
JEWISH LIGHTS Publishing
Woodstock, Vermont
www.jewishlights.com

Six Jewish Spiritual Paths:
A Rationalist Looks at Spirituality

© 2000 by Rifat Sonsino

Library of Congress Cataloging-in-Publication Data

Sonsino, Rifat, 1938–
Six Jewish spiritual paths : a rationalist looks at spiritual-
ity / Rifat Sonsino.
        p. cm.
Includes bibliographical references.
ISBN 1-58023-095-4 (hc.)
1. Spiritual life—Judaism. 2. Jewish way of life. I. Title.
BM723 .S665 2000
296.7—dc21

                                        00-010650

10 9 8 7 6 5 4 3 2 1

Manufactured in the United States of America

Jacket design by Kieran McCabe
Text design by Terry Bain

For People of All Faiths, All Backgrounds
Published by Jewish Lights Publishing
A Division of LongHill Partners, Inc.
Sunset Farm Offices, Route 4, P.O. Box 237
Woodstock, VT 05091
Tel: (802) 457-4000
Fax: (802) 457-4004
www.jewishlights.com

TO INES SONSINO
FOR HER LOVE AND SUPPORT

I Bar Kapparah expounded: Which is the brief
biblical passage upon which all the basic principles
of the Torah depend?

"In all your ways, know the divine" (Proverbs 3:6).

—Ber. 63a

Contents

Acknowledgments

THIS BOOK BEGAN as a joint venture with my colleague Rabbi Daniel B. Syme, now at Temple Beth El in Bloomfield, Michigan, but not too long after its inception, it became my own responsibility. I am very grateful to him for his initial effort.

I am very much indebted to those who have contributed to this book by providing personal testimonies. Among them, I wish to single out Michael J. Bohnen, Ina Glasberg, Rabbi Roland B. Gittelsohn *(z"l)*, Rabbi Rolando Matalon, Rabbi Paul J. Menitoff, and Rabbi Daniel B. Syme.

My deepest thanks go to the wonderful people at Jewish Lights; in particular to my publisher, Stuart Matlins, for encouraging me to proceed with my research, and to Sandra Korinchak, editorial vice-president, for her diligence, patience, and thoroughness in her editorial work. It was a pleasure to work with both of them.

I also thank Muriel Freedman and Eppie Begleiter for typing part of an earlier draft of the manuscript.

Introduction

S OME PEOPLE SAY that religion and spirituality are not exactly the same. They maintain that religion deals with prescribed acts, whereas spirituality refers to the quest for a transcendent reality. The first demands belief, whereas the second is open and fluid. Some proponents of spirituality even suggest that religion can be an impediment to communion with God by burdening the person with doctrine and ritual. Therefore, they prefer to deepen their spirituality outside of the organized religious community.

I, on the other hand, believe that religion and spirituality are interrelated. In fact, I maintain that spirituality is a powerful way to express religious yearnings. If we were to take psychoanalyst Erich Fromm's broad definition of religion, "any system of thought and action shared by a group which gives an individual a frame of orientation and an object of devotion,"[1] it would lead us to the necessary conclusion that we are all religious. This is because each of us has a different frame of orientation as well as an object of devotion. The question is how to structure this frame, and how to identify this object. Spirituality, I submit, provides the answer.

Furthermore, spirituality is not found in a vacuum. We discover our spirituality in our own cultural framework, and religion is part of that, just like language, history, and kinship ties. A Jew sees the world through Jewish eyes. Christian spirituality emerges from the Christian worldview. Moslems are heavily influenced by the Koranic perspective.

This is not to deny that people interact with one another; in fact, there is often cross-fertilization between cultures. But ultimately, each group develops, more or less, its own special path or paths to spirituality in the end, out of the influences that combine to form its cultural framework. Jews are no exception. Take, for example, the case of American and Turkish Jews. Though they live far from each other and remain under the influence of their own local cultures, they still share a similar worldview based on kinship ties as well as common history, sacred language, religious holidays and rituals. The same applies to other ethnic groups that are spread throughout the world.

The cultural diversity among nations, however, makes it more difficult for us to reach an understanding of spirituality that has universal acceptance. Many people define spirituality in rather narrow terms, limiting it to meditation or the pursuit of good deeds, for example. Others prefer a broader approach that includes various alternatives. Each attempt has its pluses and minuses. In a narrow definition, spirituality has its basis in a specific theological outlook, personal philosophy, or mode of operation. Within this definition, a person can accept spirituality or reject it according to whether it meets particular theological assumptions and practices to which the person subscribes. However, this leaves out those who might disagree with those circumscribed boundaries. A broader and more inclusive definition of spirituality is one that has a greater degree of flexibility, one that enables individuals to choose their own interpretations from among valid options. Here, within a larger framework, each path is considered authentic and can be pursued either alone or in combination with others. The drawback to this approach is that it risks being open to criticism that "anything goes."

Because there are so many different valid concepts of the divine, and consequently a variety of spiritual approaches to life, I think it is preferable to struggle with a broader definition of spirituality than to deny authenticity to many people who do not share this or that particular religious outlook. For example, people who support a narrow definition of spirituality, based on a theistic or religious-naturalistic concept of God, tend to dismiss a humanistic approach as invalid. What is their basic concern? Most likely they fear that unless things are identified clearly and narrowly, the door will be open to any kind of act beyond their level of toleration that the practitioners might call spiritual. This, in fact, happened in the seventeenth century. Sabbateanism was a splinter group of the followers of Sabbetay Zevi, the false messiah of the Jewish community in the Ottoman Empire, and those followers reportedly engaged in wife swapping during some of the religious festivals, calling it a *tikkun*—an act of repairing the world. The rest of the Jewish world simply rejected this as abhorrent behavior.

Admittedly, the broader definition does raise legitimate concerns. There will always be some people who will abuse the acceptable ethical norms in society. But that is not enough of a reason to deny others from carrying out spiritual acts, for the spiritual quest is ultimately based on the human need to find existential meaning in life, to relate to something or someone larger than the self, to relate to God as the source of all life, no matter how God is defined. This is a universal need, and there are different ways of filling it.

The solution to this dilemma, therefore, must be sought not in the black-and-white world of ideas but in the shades of gray that color our lives. It is possible to argue that some activities and

approaches are more spiritual than others. Also, some acts may
be acceptable as authentic in other religions, but not in Judaism
or by all Jews.

   This book will provide you with routes for the expression of
spirituality—routes that are legitimate within the framework of
Judaism. The various spiritual paths that are available to Jews in
their search for authentic religious expression emerge in a close
look at issues such as the meaning of spirituality, the challenges
of this quest for a modern Jew, and the sources of spirituality
within the Jewish tradition. Though this study is written from a
Jewish perspective, the spiritual paths discussed here are found
in other religions and philosophical systems, and the methodol-
ogy used here can easily be applied to the spiritual yearnings of
all of us. In struggling with these matters, some will realize that
their spiritual practices already have the ring of authenticity, and
some may seek another way for themselves. The end result will
be significant and personally enriching. Join me, then, in this
quest with an open mind and a searching heart.

CHAPTER 1

Spirituality—What Is It?

THE NEED

THE TERM *SPIRITUALITY* is very popular these days. Very often it is combined with other concepts, such as living in harmony with nature, following one's own inner voice, seeking purpose and meaning in life, searching for the Ultimate, for God. Spirituality has also been equated with the idea of transcendence, either through self-realization or in connection with the divine. The language of spirituality is now part of the regular parlance of ordinary life. People are even delving into "health care spirituality" and the "spirituality of shame."[1]

The thirst for meaning and purpose that comes after a period of personal crisis or reflection, such as the death of a loved one, has always caused people to search for spirituality. The question is this: why has our generation turned to seeking a form of transcendence so diligently? Why now? Many reasons come to mind, for example, the realization that science cannot solve all our problems and a resulting disappointment with our technology-oriented life; the precarious life we live under the constant threat of war, violence, and tragedy; and the understanding that we are not the center of the universe as we experience the world becoming "smaller" thanks to global communication.

The quest for spirituality is a universal phenomenon. Contrary to popular belief, it is not limited to Eastern religions. And while some are seeking religious renewal outside the faith of their birth, many others are searching for higher levels of awakening within their own religious framework.

Jews are part of this search as well, and have been for a long time. And now they too are seeking spirituality with great fervor. There may be particular reasons for this renewed interest. Rabbi Michael Lerner, the editor of *Tikkun* and one of the contemporary leaders of the Jewish Renewal movement, notes, "It is no wonder that after having faced massive and staggering destruction and dislocations, many Jews feel spiritually and emotionally dead.... It has taken many decades for Jews to feel secure enough to begin to renew the spiritual tradition."[2] Rabbi Arthur Green of Brandeis University suggests a related factor: "the high level of material success that many have attained over the course of these four generations."[3] This point is highlighted in the *Utne Reader* as an example of a lack of spirituality in our media and popular culture; Bill McKibben writes, "For a long time in our lives, materialism was more fun. Why? Because we didn't have much stuff. We lived on the farm or in the slum, we lived through the Depression, our material lives were pretty bleak.... But here, the middle and upper classes have reached a saturation point where new things no longer provide an added increment of pleasure."[4]

Many contemporary Jews, however, find Judaism wanting in spirituality. Though they strongly identify with the cultural aspects of Judaism, they find that Jewish religious practices inhibit their quest. "I am a cultural Jew, not a religious Jew," they say. Reb Zalman Schachter-Shalomi, one of the most important leaders of the Jewish Renewal movement today, writes, "Jews everywhere are on a quest motivated by a malaise, a feeling that there must be more in Judaism than the cut-and-dried version frequently encountered in contemporary services. The seeker [is] in search of a way to express spiritual stirrings, and a practical method with which [to] develop that holy source within so that it will begin to flow freely."⁵ Similarly, Dr. David Ariel, president of the Cleveland College of Jewish Studies, says, "Many of us do not find our faith to be a significant factor in our lives or a compelling guide to life today. We search, often in vain, for a spiritual home in Judaism. Our spiritual aspirations are often high, but Judaism does not seem to be sufficiently spiritual…. We feel Jewish, but we find it difficult to put that feeling into words."⁶

In the last few years, many inquisitive Jews have in fact sought spiritual enlightenment in Eastern religions or in the meditative spiritual techniques of foreign cultures. Today it is not uncommon, for example, for Israeli young men and women to leave Israel after army service to travel in the Far East in search of transcendental experiences,⁷ often in order to find an alternative to rigid Orthodoxy in Israel. Many have explored Buddhist teachings, and some have even left the Jewish religion altogether. But others have remained Jews, though Buddhism heavily influences their religious beliefs. These so-called JUBUs (Jewish-Buddhists) do not see Judaism and Buddhism as incompatible. In fact, it is the congruence of the two approaches that brought many of them to conclude that they can be both at the same time.

However, there is no need for a Jew to seek spirituality by looking elsewhere in other cultures. Judaism has a very rich spiritual tradition of its own. This is not to deny that other societies lack religious fervor or that they cannot enrich our own quest. Judaism has frequently incorporated elements from the surrounding cultures into its own fabric, and is open to inquiries from any searching mind.

Today, the quest for spirituality is a high educational priority in almost every Jewish institution. Whereas social action used to be at the head of the Jewish community's agenda, it is

spirituality that now occupies center stage in response to our society's high premium on individuality. Jews want to know what
it means to be Jewish in the twenty-first century. How does being
Jewish affect me as an individual? To meet this ever-increasing
need, many rabbis and educators have started to talk more about
God, faith, and the meaning of life in Judaism. Classes and seminars are now being conducted throughout the Jewish world on
religious subjects, as people recognize the limits of pure ratio-
nalism as the basis of contemporary Judaism and want something more. And many Jews are responding favorably. Through
weekend retreats, adult education seminars, and intensive community educational programs, significant numbers of Jews from
San Francisco to Sydney are studying about Jewish history, customs, ceremonies, values, and beliefs. The path of Jewish mysticism and, particularly, the study of the *Zohar*, the masterpiece of
Spanish Kabbalism of the thirteenth century, are particularly
popular topics of discussion in synagogues and community fo-
rums. Universities are offering classes on general Jewish topics
and even Kabbalah to an ever-increasing student population,
both Jewish and non-Jewish. Some people are meeting in living
rooms to study mysticism with private teachers. In many areas,
Kabbalah has even reached the masses: In Tel Aviv, the Kabbalah
Learning Center has a display in the central bus station.

What is presently needed is for seekers to look for and find
legitimate avenues of spirituality in Judaism, being careful to
avoid viewing one single path as the only valid approach.
Regrettably, some thinkers have in the past promoted—and many
still do—this kind of path by pointing, for example, to Kabbalah
or mysticism as the exclusive way. There is no doubt that the
mystical approach is a legitimate way to experience spirituality,
but it is not the only possible one within Judaism.

It is important that whichever spiritual avenue a person
chooses for himself or herself, it should not only meet the needs
of the heart but also be compatible with reason. As Rabbi Karyn

D. Kedar, the Great Lakes Regional Director of the Union of American Hebrew Congregations and author on spirituality, warns us, "Beware of the spiritual path if it does not invite the mind to gauge its sense of reality."[8]

CHALLENGES TO SPIRITUALITY

While many struggle with the terms and content of spirituality, some Jewish thinkers strongly argue just the opposite. They claim that spirituality, by itself, is antithetical to Judaism. To many Jews, spirituality evokes monastic life, otherworldliness, and the awesome silences of dark cathedrals, so alien to the values and experiences of many Jews.[9] No wonder some of the reactions are very strong. "I do not require 'spirituality,'" writes Rabbi Harry Essrig, the publisher of *The American Rabbi*. "It is enough that I have Judaism. If more Jews attended Sabbath services, if more Jews observed the beautiful rituals of our faith, if more Jews attended adult education classes, if more participated in the struggle for social justice, would we not have a superabundance of 'spirituality'?"[10]

Other Jewish thinkers who are critical of this spiritual quest fear that focusing on nonworldly matters will severely limit our ability to deal with pressing everyday issues. Francine Klagsbrun, an author and a Jewish activist, warns that spirituality must not become "a substitute for the rigors of scholarship, for wrestling with reality, for struggling with the nitty-grittiness of existence."[11]

In a similar vein, others fear that spirituality will take people away from their involvement in social action. "Certainly I am not opposed to any effort that will bring our people closer to God and His kingdom, but I would like to see some of this aggressiveness and zeal applied to *tikkun olam*, the repair of society, as well,"[12] writes Rabbi Harold L. Gelfman of Jacksonville, Florida. Then he adds, "One of the greatest fears I have about this 'spirituality' is that it makes us believe that our problems can be solved by simplistic solutions, by the right attitude, by the right words.... Spirituality in our day is a subtle form of assimilation."[13]

Charles S. Liebman, a prominent writer, questions the validity of spirituality as an appropriate religious orientation: "Spirituality is not the answer to the Jewish problem. Spirituality is the problem." He adds, "We are commanded to be a 'holy,' not a 'spiritual' people, and the *musar* [Jewish ethical writings] literature is concerned with holiness, not spirituality." He advances three major objections to this trend: (1) Its informality borders on the "leisure-time...that includes chatting with God." (2) Its egalitarianism ends with the "reification of selected attributes of the individual himself." (3) Its ethical ideals are based on the proper intention and ignore the requirements of the rituals that are to be carried out according to custom and law. Liebman concludes by saying that spirituality "substitutes a Judaism focused upon the legitimation of self." As such, it is "a recipe for disaster."[14]

Dr. Michael Chernick, professor of Talmud at the Hebrew Union College–Jewish Institute of Religion, expresses concern about what he calls "warm fuzzies spirituality,"[15] which, he says, is narcissistic in nature and reduces God to a source of personal pleasure. Still other critics question whether spirituality is an authentic Jewish value, arguing that it reflects a dualistic approach to the human being—divine soul and earthly body—which is more Greek and Christian than biblical and rabbinic. These critics maintain that such a dualism, at the very core, implies a debasement of the human body, claiming that it is nothing but a prison for the nonmaterial spirit.[16]

True, the Greek and Christian views of spirituality are based on dualistic thinking, but that does not necessarily mean that Judaism is devoid of spirituality altogether or that it has to be defined in Greek and Christian terms. As we shall explore, it can be argued that an authentic Jewish spirituality is indeed rooted in Jewish sources and is compatible with Jewish thinking. It can satisfactorily meet the needs of Jews today. Unquestionably, all the caveats mentioned above must be taken seriously, but they do not warrant an avoidance of the spiritual quest, which is rooted, I believe, in the human need to transcend oneself in search of answers to life's existential questions.

Any kind of exclusionist approach will turn off those of us who cannot, on the basis of thought or practice, sign onto a particular spiritual path and will cause us to feel as if we are not legitimate within the system. In reality, Judaism has a rich tradition of spirituality and provides distinct avenues of religious expression that can nourish the soul and satisfy the needs of the mind as well. Where do we find these answers?

JEWISH DEFINITIONS OF SPIRITUALITY

Though spirituality is popularly discussed in many sources, there is no clear definition of this term. It has become like a buzzword, dealing in general with liturgy, ritual, study, meditation, community, social justice, and certainly God. Rabbi Jeffrey J. Weisblatt (z"l) of Temple Ohev Shalom in Harrisburg, Pennsylvania, put it succinctly: "There is no one definition for it."[17]

Although not all Jewish thinkers agree on a definition of spirituality, several have been proposed. Here are a few examples:

- "Spirituality may inclusively be regarded as the sum of the efforts of the human psyche, individually and collectively, to attune to the impulses and rhythms of the universe, whether internal to the individual or external in nature."[18] (Dr. Martin A. Cohen, Hebrew Union College–Jewish Institute of Religion)

- "Man's spiritual life can easily be thought of in three divisions: his pursuit of truth, of beauty, and of moral goodness."[19] (Rabbi Roland B. Gittelsohn [1910–1995], Temple Israel, Boston)

- "Spirituality, as I understand it, is noticing the wonder, noticing that what seems disparate and confusing to us is actually whole."[20] (Rabbi Nancy Fuchs-Kreimer, Reconstructionist Rabbinical College, Philadelphia)

- "The striving for life in the presence of God and the fashioning of a life of holiness appropriate to such striving."[21] (Rabbi Arthur Green, Brandeis University, Boston)

- "The cognitive and/or behavioral activities designed to help individual and community to reconnect to God."[22] (Deanne H. Shapiro and Johanna Shapiro, psychologists at the University of California, Irvine)

- "The immediacy of God's presence."[23] (Rabbi Lawrence Kushner, Rabbi-in-Residence, Hebrew Union College–Jewish Institute of Religion)

- "Spirituality is essentially a way of responding to God, becoming conscious of God."[24] (Rabbi Jeffrey J. Weisblatt [d. 1995], Temple Ohev Shalom, Harrisburg, Pennsylvania)

- "Spirituality is the process through which the individual strives to meet God."[25] (Rabbi Kerry M. Olitzky, Jewish Outreach Institute, New York)

- "A highly personal outlook about what is sacred about us; it is the expression of our most deeply held values, and it is that sense of higher purpose that guides our daily lives."[26] (Dr. David S. Ariel, Cleveland College of Jewish Studies)

We can see that these definitions are not that different from one another and that they share connections. My personal preference is to define spirituality as broadly as possible, seeing in it an overarching experience involving our search for meaning and purpose in life.[27]

Spirituality is an act of will as well as a process. But primarily it is a state of mind. It can—and should—lead to action and often does, but basically it elevates our spirit and makes us more aware of ourselves and the place we occupy in life. Ultimately, it brings us closer to God as the source of our existence. Living a spiritual life enables us to reach a comprehensive and integrative sense of our purpose and role in life—in effect, mindfully placing ourselves in God's universe suffused with God's wonders. I define spirituality as simply "the awareness of standing before God," no matter how the term *God* is defined within the larger Jewish tradition, and whether or not God can be "met," "experienced," or "felt." In this definition I hear an echo of the text on top of many synagogue Torah arks: "Know before whom you stand" (Ber. 28b). When we really "know"—in the sense of reaching an intimate inner transformation, as in the Hebrew term *da'at* ("knowledge")—that we are standing before the Ultimate Source of Reality, we are filled with awe and wonder, and we consequently respond to the divine and to the reality that surrounds us with an open heart and total commitment.

TERMINOLOGY

In modern Hebrew, the term spirituality is usually rendered as *ruhaniyut*. This word is based on the Hebrew word *ruah*, which is frequently combined or used with two other Hebrew words: *nefesh* and *neshamah*. Over the course of time, these words have become almost synonymous, meaning "spirit" or "soul." In the past, however, these terms had more restricted meanings. To gain a better understanding of spirituality in Judaism today, it is appropriate to survey the development of these words in the Jewish sacred texts over the centuries.

Ruah

The root meaning of *ruah* is "wind" or "a movement of air." For example, when Moses in one of his confrontations with the

Pharaoh held out his rod over the land of Egypt, the Bible tells us that God drove an "east wind" *(ruah kadim)* over the land all day and all night (Exodus 10:13).²⁸ Similarly, according to the Book of Proverbs, "A north wind *[ruah tzafon]* produces rain" (25:23). It is also in this sense that we read, at the beginning of creation, that "a wind from God" *(ruah Elohim)* swept over the water (Genesis 1:2).

The word *ruah*, by extension, also means "breath." Thus, God tells Noah, "I am about to bring the Flood...to destroy all flesh under the sky in which there is the breath of life" *(ruah hayyim)* (Genesis 6:17). In the Book of Job, one of Job's companions, Eliphaz, says that the wicked person shall "pass away by the breath of His mouth" *(ruah piv)* (15:30). Job himself complains that "My odor [literally, 'my breath,' *ruhi*] is offensive to my wife" (19:17).

The word *ruah* also refers to "prophetic spirit." For instance, when the disciples of Elisha saw him crossing the Jordan, they shouted, "The spirit of Elijah *[ruah Eliyahu]* has settled on Elisha" (II Kings 2:15). When Joseph was able to interpret the Pharaoh's dreams to the king's satisfaction, the Pharaoh asked his courtiers, "Could we find another like him [namely, Joseph], a man in whom is the spirit of God *[ruah Elohim]*?" (Genesis 41:38).

The word *ruah* frequently means "spirit" in the sense of disposition, vigor, temper, courage. Thus, for example, during the days of Joshua, when the local kings heard what God had done on behalf of the Israelites, "they lost heart, and no spirit *(ruah)* was left in them" (Joshua 5:10). The Book of Proverbs praises the one who has "self-control" *(moshel ruho)* (16:32). After Pharaoh's second dream, the Bible tells us, he woke up because "his spirit *(ruho)* was agitated" (Genesis 41:8).

In the rabbinic period, the sages expanded the definition of *ruah* to include demons as well. Thus, for example, we find in the Talmud the following statement: "R. Jeremiah b. Eleazar stated: In all those years [after his expulsion from the Garden of Eden] during which Adam was under the ban, he begot ghosts *(ruhin)* and male and female demons" (Erub. 18b). Centuries later, in Spain, the medieval Jewish philosopher Moses Maimonides (1125–1204) used the term to mean "intellect," "purpose," or will."[29] In modern Hebrew, *ruah* combines most of these meanings and refers to "wind," "spirit," or "mind."

Nefesh

Another Hebrew term connoting "spirit" is *nefesh*, a word related to the Akkadian *napishtu* or Ugaritic *npsh*, meaning "throat." (A trace of this original definition can be found in Psalms 105:28: "an iron collar was put on his neck" *[nafsho].*)

In time, by extension, the term came to mean "a living being," "the person himself/herself." Thus, for instance, in Job 12:10, we read: "In His hand is every living soul [literally, 'being,' *nefesh kol hai*]." Similarly, when God blew into Adam's nostrils the breath of life, he became a "living being" *(nefesh hayyah)* (Genesis 2:7). Speaking about his sons Simeon and Levi, Jacob prayed, "Let not my person *(nafshi)* be included in their assembly" (Genesis 49:6). In the Book of Leviticus, many laws begin with the words "If a person…" *(nefesh ki...)* (Leviticus 5:1, 2, 4, 15, 17, 20, etc.). The word *nefesh* can sometimes best be translated as "life." For example, when someone murders another, the penalty is "life for life" *(nefesh tahat nefesh)* (Exodus 21:23).

In certain contexts, the word *nefesh* also refers to human feelings, as, for example, in Exodus 23:9, where the law tells us not to oppress the stranger, "for you know the feelings *[nefesh]* of the stranger." When paired with a qualifying adjective, *nefesh* is used at times to express the fulfillment of basic human needs, such as "For He has satisfied the thirsty *[nefesh shokekah]*, filled the hungry *[venefesh r'evah]* with all good things" (Psalms 107:9).

In rabbinic literature, *nefesh* took on the additional meaning of "soul," "desire," "will," and even "a resting place," "a cemetery monument." Many medieval Jewish philosophers used it in the sense of "rational soul." In modern Hebrew, *nefesh* is a general term for "soul," "spirit," "person," "self," "mind," "will," "tomb," and so on.

Neshamah

In the Bible the basic meaning of *neshamah* is "breath," very much like *ruah*. Thus, in the Book of Isaiah, we read, "Oh, cease to glorify man, who has only a breath *[neshamah]* in his nostrils" (2:22). Very often, this word is used synonymously with *nefesh,* as in Joshua 11:11, "They proscribed and put to the sword every person *[nefesh]* in it. Not a soul [literally, 'a person,' *neshamah*] survived." At times, it appears in combination with the word *ruah,* as in Genesis 7:22, where we are told that during the Flood the devastation was so great that "All in whose nostrils was the merest breath of life *[nishmat ruah]* died."

The word *neshamah* also refers to the divine vital principle that makes an individual a person. Thus, for example, when God created Adam, God blew into his nostrils "the breath of life" *(nishmat hayyim),* and he became a human being (Genesis 2:7). Similarly, according to the Book of Proverbs, "the life breath of man *[nishmat adam]* is the lamp of the Lord" (20:27). In rabbinic literature, the word means "a person" but also an independent "soul." In modern Hebrew, *neshamah* refers to "soul," "spirit," or "life" and often has the connotation of "a good person."

Nefesh, Ruah, and Neshamah as Levels of the Soul

For some Jewish thinkers, each of these three terms for spirit or soul plays a special role in the development of a human being. According to the *Zohar, nefesh, ruah,* and *neshamah,* collectively called NaRaN, form a sequence from lower to higher: *nefesh* enters at the time of birth and is the source of vitality; *ruah* is postnatal and is aroused when a person is able to surmount purely physical desires; and *neshamah*, the highest of the three, is developed when a person engages in Torah and its commandments and "opens his higher power of apprehension, especially his ability to mystically apprehend the Godhead and the secrets of the Universe."[30] And according to this hierarchy, "At death, the *nefesh* remains in the grave, lamenting over the death of the body. The *ruah* ascends to whatever level of celestial paradise it has earned by the merits it has accrued, and the *neshamah* goes directly back to the fullness of God."[31]

For Rabbi Wayne Dosick—teacher and author, and spiritual guide of the Elijah Minyan in San Diego—the soul has not three but five different levels, radiating from the innermost to the outermost level, which is the level of union with God. *Nefesh* represents the physical being, *ruah* stands for the qualities of our uniqueness, and *neshamah*, separating us from animals, reflects our ability to think, reason, and remember. Here Rabbi Dosick adds two more levels: *hayyah* is our life force, and *yehidah* is our intuition, "where the singular, unique oneness of each soul crosses the abyss and knows that there is no distance to *Yachid*, the Infinite Oneness of God."[32]

The shades of meaning of these three Hebrew words—*ruah, nefesh,* and *neshamah*—point to the emphasis in Jewish thought and tradition that a human being is more than a physical entity. There is in him or her an invisible element described by the Jewish mystics as a divine spark that enables every individual to aspire for something greater than the self. This assertion is the basis of any kind of spirituality.

THE JEWISH PATHS TO SPIRITUALITY

"The impulse behind the new spirituality," writes Rabbi Neil Gillman, Professor of Jewish Philosophy at The Jewish Theological Seminary in New York, "is the primacy of feeling."[33]

Obviously, the experience of spirituality is a highly personal matter. What appeals to one individual does not always appeal to another. Two people who experience the same event may respond in opposite ways: one considers it as highly spiritual, whereas the other feels it as inconsequential. There cannot be one type of spirituality that is valid for everybody. Life experiences show us that there are various types of spirituality, just as there are different kinds of people.

Authentic Jewish spiritual expression takes different forms. Whether one chooses to explore it through acts of transcendence, study, prayer, meditation, or relationships and good deeds, each alternative expression, practiced separately or with the others, must be considered an authentic expression of Jewish commitment.[34]

Furthermore, these paths of spirituality are not mutually exclusive. In other words, a person who expresses his or her spirituality primarily through Torah study can also, on other occasions and under different circumstances, experience a spiritual high through a good deed or during a meditation session. An insight obtained during prayer may lead an individual to carry out a *mitzvah* for another human being. A religious ritual may at times elevate one's soul to great spiritual heights. As spiritual experiences these special moments are like roads that intersect at some points and then separate from one another. They may be practiced one after the other. One person may prefer to combine two or three together. They are like pentimento, wherein one image in a painting overlies an earlier image but does not obliterate it. They are like fabrics in which one shade of color is interwoven with another. We are not dealing here with parallel lines of spirituality but with paths that often meet in an upward movement toward a Light that uplifts the spirit and makes one whole.

It is said that Rabbi Menahem Mendel of Kotzk once asked his students, "Where does God dwell?" Thinking the answer obvious, one of them said, "God dwells everywhere!" "No," said the Rabbi, "God dwells wherever we let God in." Each person must do this according to his or her own personal needs and disposition.

The challenge for the modern Jew is to understand these paths, to assimilate them, and then to choose, out of the plethora of Jewish ideas, the approach to spirituality that best expresses a sense of personal transcendence.

Where can we find these Jewish sources? What are the alternatives open to us in Jewish spiritual expression? In the next chapters we discuss some of these paths in greater detail.

The Jewish Spiritual Quest from Biblical Times to the Present: A Historical Survey

FROM THE EARLIEST TIMES of our people's history, Jewish sages have tried to meet the spiritual needs of their contemporaries. They have emphasized belief in one God, sought to deepen the people's sense of wonder, and stressed the need to behave in an ethical manner. They also have preserved old rituals and, when necessary, created new ones to address the religious yearnings and existential questions of the individual and the community. Their answers vary significantly from period to period and often reflect the prevailing mindset of the time. These teachings, scattered as they are throughout Jewish literature, lack systematization. However, by surveying the various periods of history, we can identify some patterns in the ways in which Jews have understood spirituality.

IN THE BIBLE

The idea that a person is composed of a body and a soul has its roots primarily in ancient Greek thought. In the biblical view, body and soul are one and the same. As one scholar put it, an individual "does not have a soul, he is a soul."[1] According to another, "The whole of man is a living soul."² Each person is a *nefesh hayyah,* a living being (Genesis 2:7).

The Biblical world was different from ours with regard to the role attributed to various organs in the human body. For example, we now think of the brain as the seat of the mind, and the heart as the central organ for emotions. We say, "He is a brainy kid" and " I love you with all my heart." That was not the case in ancient Israel: The heart (Hebrew, *lev*) was considered the primary seat of the mind, and emotions lay in the bowels, or the internal organs, primarily the kidneys. Thus, the prophet Jeremiah calls one "devoid of intelligence" as *en lev* (5:21); a person without a sense or mind is known as *hasar lev* ("devoid of sense," Proverbs 6:32). Consequently, when we read in Deuteronomy 6:5, "You shall love the Lord your God with all your heart *(levavekha),*" it really means with your intellectual ability.³ On the other hand, when the prophet wants to express emotions, he writes,

> Truly, Ephraim is a dear son to Me,
>
> A child that is dandled!
>
> Whenever I have turned against him,
>
> My thoughts would dwell on him still.
>
> That is why My heart [*meay,* literally, "my internal organs"] yearns for him.
>
> (Jeremiah 31:20)

Similarly, the author of the Book of Proverbs writes, "I will rejoice with all my heart [literally, "my kidneys," *khilyotay*]" (23:16), or Job says, "My heart [literally, "my kidneys," *khilyotay*] pines within me" (19:27).

In order to understand the role of spirituality within the ancient world, not only do we have to contend with different vocabulary, meanings, and usages, but we also need to remember that the ancient Near East, including Israel, did not know secularism. This was a society totally immersed in religion. Everyone assumed belief in God. Everything was under the providence of the divinity. "The fool says in his heart, 'there is no god,'" writes the psalmist (14:1; 53:2). The challenge for the leaders of Israel was to keep the people away from idolatry and the worship of other gods.

On the basis of biblical and ancient Near Eastern texts as well as various archaeological findings, we can deduce that in ancient Israel religious expressions took place within the community, especially within the Temple of Jerusalem through an elaborate sacrificial system directed by a large cadre of priests. The Temple was the cultural, economic, and legal center of the community, and to it each Israelite came to commune with God, through the mediation of a priest, and to obtain atonement and a blessing.

During the year, individual Jews made pilgrimages to Jerusalem, primarily during the three major harvest festivals—Passover (Pesah), Weeks (Shavuot) and Tabernacles (Sukkot)—to offer sacrifices and, on occasion, to recite prescribed blessings (compare, for example, Deuteronomy 26:5ff.; Psalms 66:13). Among the highest gifts an individual could receive was the opportunity to "dwell in the house of the Lord for many long years" (Psalms 23:6; 27:4; 65:5; 84:5).

To show devotion to God, an Israelite was expected to love as well to fear God. Psalms 31:24 states, "Love the Lord, all you faithful," which is echoed in Deuteronomy 6:5. On the other hand, we have several passages in which a person is asked to "fear God" (Leviticus 19:14, 32; 25:36, 43). At times, both of these emotions are combined in one statement, as if each stood for one side of the same coin. Thus, according to the Book of Deuteronomy, God asks each Israelite "to revere [literally, 'to fear'] the Lord your God, to walk only in His paths, to love Him, and to serve the Lord your God" (10:12).

The concept of love of God, viewed in its literary and

historical context, basically means to be loyal to God. Thus, as one scholar wrote, "The love that God commands from Israel is not primarily a matter of intimate affection, but is to be expressed by obedience to God's commandments, serving God, showing reverence for God, and being loyal to God alone."[4] Dr. Jeffrey H. Tigay, author of the *JPS Commentary on Deuteronomy* and my Bible teacher, remarks that in Deuteronomy, God's love for human beings is expressed in benevolent acts and that Israel's duty to *love* God means to observe the commandments diligently and lovingly. He writes, "The command to love God [Deuteronomy 6:5] may accordingly be understood as requiring to act lovingly and loyally toward Him."[5] As many scholars have already noted, the term *love* here has a legal connotation. It derives from the political treaties of the ancient Near East, where the overlord asks the vassal to love him— namely, to be loyal to him—by not rebelling or taking the side of the enemy. For example, in a vassal treaty of Esarhaddon (680–669 B.C.E.) of Assyria, the king tells his subordinate, "If you do not love the crown prince designate Ashurbanipal…as you do your own lives…may…[curses follow here]."[6] In the biblical context, too, the expression "loving God" means serving God exclusively and carrying out God's commands diligently.

On the other hand, the "fear of God" according to the Bible is "the beginning of wisdom" (Psalms 111:10) as well as "the beginning of knowledge" (Proverbs 1:7). It is more than simple reverence and piety. It connotes a kind of awesomeness. God requires absolute and exclusive worship. Those who loyally carry out God's commandments are rewarded with blessings; those who ignore them are cursed and punished. Thus, we read: "If you follow My laws and faithfully observe My commandments, I will grant your rains in their season.… But if you do not obey Me and do not observe all these commandments…I will wreak misery upon you" (Leviticus 26:3–16ff.).

In the seventh century B.C.E., during the days of King Josiah of Judah, local temples dedicated to YHVH were destroyed, and the

Temple of Jerusalem became the only central institution for all cultic functions. The biblical texts make no allusion to any prayers being recited during the offering of the sacrifices at this time. Most likely, the action was carried out in silence. Things changed during the second Temple period, when prayers, blessings, and scriptural readings were added to the daily service. With the destruction of the Temple in 70 C.E. by the Romans, the sacrificial cult finally gave way to new forms of religious practices, thus broadening spiritual expression, including the performance of biblical and rabbinic *mitzvot* (literally "commandments") as well as the recital of individual and community prayers.

A rabbinic source tells us that,

> Once as Rabban Johanan ben Zakkai was coming from Jerusalem, Rabbi Joshua followed after him and saw the Temple in ruins. "Woe unto us!" Rabbi Joshua cried, "that this, the place where the iniquities of Israel were atoned for, is laid waste!" "My son," Rabban Johanan said to him, "be not grieved; we have another atonement as effective as this. And what is it? It is acts of loving-kindness, as it is said, 'For I desire mercy and not sacrifice' (Hosea 6:6)." (Avot de Rabbi Natan, ch. 6)

Similarly, we are told, Rabbi Isaac said:

> We have now no prophet or priest or sacrifices or Temple, or altar which can make atonement for us: from the day whereon the Temple was laid waste, nothing was left for us but prayer. (Midrash on Psalms, on 5:4)

IN THE RABBINIC PERIOD

Toward the end of the first century C.E., the synagogue appeared as an established religious institution under the leadership of the rabbinic sages.[7] After the cessation of sacrifices and the destruction of the Temple by the Romans in the year 70 C.E., the Rabbis' creation of the prayer structure became the primary means for expressing religious devotion. The old sacrificial service called *avodah* ("service") now simply meant "the service of the heart."

The synagogue was a radically different place from the Temple of Jerusalem. There, a hereditary priestly caste had led the prescribed rituals. The *kohanim* (priest) and *levi'im* (Levites) occupied a higher place in the operation of Temple functions; the ordinary Jew had a rather limited role in the service. In the synagogue, however, there was no priestly domination. True, the titles *kohen* and *levi* were preserved out of respect for those who had held high positions in the Temple structure; furthermore, these former priests were now accorded certain privileges in the synagogue. But it was made clear to all that anyone could study Torah and become a leader in the synagogue, which quickly evolved into a house of worship *(bet t'fillah)* and a house of study *(bet midrash)* as well as a house of meeting *(bet k'nesset)*. Not lineage but knowledge was now the determining factor as to who became a leader.

To enable the Israelites to express their religion, the rabbis began to create prayers for special occasions. At the beginning, there was a great deal of fluidity in this area, but slowly a regular pattern emerged. The rabbis insisted, however, that prayers require preparation and especially proper intention and concentration *(kavanah)*. The Talmud is very clear about it: "Prayer needs *kavanah*" (J. Ber. 4:1). However, for the ancient rabbis, the synagogue was not the only sacred place where prayers can be recited. Invoking God, they taught,

> I bade you pray in the synagogue in your city, but if you cannot pray there, pray in your field, and if you cannot pray there, pray on your bed, and if you cannot pray there, then meditate in your heart and be still. (Pes. K. 158a)

In contrast to the biblical viewpoint, many rabbinic texts reflect the ancient Greek idea that the physical body is transitory and perishable, whereas the soul represents the pure element of a person's being. The soul comes pure from God. It is sinless. As one rabbinic source has it, "She belongs to the world above" (Eccles. R. 6, #6). According to a famous rabbinic prayer,

My God, the soul that you have created is a pure one.

You have created it within me.

You have breathed it into me;

You guard it within me;

One day, You will take it from me,

And restore it to me in time to come.

So long as the soul is within me,

I will give thanks to you, O Lord, my God,

And God of my ancestors.

Blessed are You, O Lord, who restores souls to dead corpses.

(Ber. 60b)

However, the rabbis do not view the body without considering the soul at the same time. "There is [on earth] no soul without a body, and no body without a soul" (Tanh. B. Vayikra 4a), they say. The destructive aspects of the inclination to do evil, the *yetzer ra*, are not ascribed solely to the body. The soul plays a role too. Furthermore, the body is a divine creation and requires daily care. In a famous rabbinic story, we are told that Hillel the elder was asked by his disciples, "Where are you going?" He answered: "To do a good deed." "What is that?" they said. "To take a bath," Hillel replied. They added, "Is this a pious deed?" He responded:

Yes, for if the man who is appointed to polish and wash
the images of the kings which are set up in the theatres and

circuses receives his rations for doing so, and is even raised up to be regarded as among the great ones of the kingdom, how much more so is it obligatory on me to polish and wash my body, since I have been created in the divine image and likeness (Genesis 9:6). (Lev. R. Behar 34:3)

At the end, both body and soul are punished or rewarded together, as is indicated by the following rabbinic teaching:

In the world to come, God says to the soul, "Why have you sinned before Me?" The soul replies: "I have not sinned; the body has sinned; since I have come out of the body, I have flown about like an innocent bird in the air; what is my sin?" Then God says to the body, "Why have you sinned before Me?" The body replies, "I have not sinned; it is the soul which has sinned; from the hour that the soul went out of me, I lie like a stone cast upon the ground. How can I have sinned against you?" What does God do? He brings the soul and casts it into the body, and judges the two together. (Lev. R. 4:5)

The sages of the rabbinic period, although very much concerned about the inner life of the individual, also concentrated their efforts on the performance of *mitzvot* as a means of expressing religious fervor. These consisted of the oral rules and regulations that govern the daily life of the individual and community, rules they believed were revealed by God on Mt. Sinai *(Torah she-be' al pe),* along with all the commandments found in the written Torah *(Torah she-bikhtav),* and therefore binding on every Jew.

Eventually the rabbis codified all of these obligations into a list of 613 *mitzvot.* Some of these deal with ethical matters; others with ritual observances. In the eyes of the rabbinic sages, one is not more important than the other, and at times it is difficult to distinguish clearly between the two. So, individual Jews are expected to carry them out with similar commitment. Not all of these *mitzvot,* however, are observable today by all Jews. Some can be carried out only within the ancient Temple of Jerusalem, and others exclusively in the land of Israel. There are *mitzvot* imposed on men and not women, and others on women but not men.

"The underlying assumption of rabbinic spirituality," writes Robert Goldenberg of the State University of New York at Stony Brook, "is that true obedience to God, true fulfillment of Israel's covenant obligations, means acceptance of and submission to this law: determining as precisely as possible the proper rule for governing action in every conceivable situation and then acting according to this rule."[8] He calls this approach the "spirituality of legalism."[9] Today, Orthodox Jews still believe that the *mitzvot* are binding because of their divine source. Non-Orthodox Jews, on the other hand, consider them to be sanctified ways of Jewish expression—divinely inspired, perhaps, but not divinely ordained and therefore open to reinterpretation, redefinition, and acceptance based on informed personal choice.[10]

IN JEWISH HELLENISTIC THOUGHT

The Jewish philosopher Philo Judaeus of Alexandria in Egypt (20 B.C.E. to 50 C.E.) was strongly influenced by Greek philosophy, in particular by the ideas of Plato. In an effort to make Judaism relevant for his contemporaries, he attempted to harmonize Judaism with the prevailing Greek thought of his time.

Like other Jewish thinkers of his time, Philo believed in the unity of God, but he argued that God is far above and beyond the physical universe. God, as the "soul" of the universe, is the cause of everything there is, and remains totally incomprehensible to the human mind. The gap between the infinite and perfect God and the imperfect and finite world of people and matter is filled by the personified *logos* (Greek for "word" or "speech"). It is through the agency of the *logos* that God operates in the world.

The biblical text, for Philo, contained a deeper meaning than its surface reading, a meaning that can be understood only when the text is interpreted allegorically. For example, when Abraham, representing the mind, marries Hagar, meaning a school, the result is poor knowledge: Ishmael, their son. But when the mind (Abraham) finds wisdom (Sarah), the result is pure joy (Isaac).

Here Abraham stands for any virtue-loving mind searching for the true God. In fact, for Philo, a contemplative life is the highest achievement of a human being. He argued that a person is composed of two basic elements, body and soul, and that the rational soul connects the individual to God. Being a mystic, he added that in order to achieve communion with God—at least with that aspect of God represented by the *logos*—one needs to deliver himself/herself from the burdens of the physical body and engage in theoretical contemplation. He stressed that a life dedicated to solitude and the pursuit of the mind is richer and certainly more rewarding than a life spent performing daily chores.

IN MEDIEVAL THOUGHT

In the medieval period, under both Greek and Muslim influence, the inner life of the individual became a prominent topic of discussion among Jewish thinkers. The perfection of the soul, they stressed, is the primary goal of human life, for it is the soul that connects us to the Divine, which is "pure spirit."

During this period, many Jewish philosophers wrote about their intense, mystical love of God and their longing for communion with the Divine. This could be achieved, according to some, through rational speculation (for example, Saadia ben Yosef [892–942] or Maimonides [1135–1204]) or by means of *devekut* (literally, "cleaving" to God). For Joseph Albo (1380–1444), "Belief in God and His Torah brings man to eternal happiness and causes his soul to cleave to the spiritual substance."[11] According to Bahya ibn Pakuda (early twelfth century C.E.), "the soul's longing…for her Creator, to cleave to His supernal light"[12] can be achieved by abstinence from worldly things and ultimately through God's highest gift of light.

The term *spirituality (ruhaniyut)* began to appear in many medieval Jewish texts. However, its meaning was very different from that of its modern counterpart. Under the influence of Greek and Muslim philosophers, many Jewish thinkers used this word basically to refer to the world of magic and spiritual beings, including angels or demons, just as some early rabbinic sages had previously done. Thus, for example, Judah Halevi, a well-known Spanish Jewish scholar of the eleventh century, made extensive use of this expression in his famous book *The Kuzari*, in the sense of "supernatural beings" (1:79), often in association with "talismans" (4:23), even referring to "the spiritual influence of some stars" (1:97) and to "the worshipers of spirits" (3:23). Similarly, the great Jewish philosopher Moses Maimonides spoke of a pagan prophet who claimed that "a particular star causes its spirituality *(ruhaniyuto)* upon me" *(Introduction to the Mishneh Torah)*. Nahmanides, a thirteenth-century Jewish thinker, mentions "the spiritual sciences" *(hokhmot ruhaniyot)*, referring to "demons, sorcery and the varieties of incense offered to the heavenly host."[13]

IN JEWISH MYSTICISM AND HASIDISM

Mysticism has been variously defined. Basically it is a philosophy that puts a high emphasis on the immediate awareness of the relation of a human being with God. Mystics crave communion with the Divine through prayer, meditation, or song. In its extreme case, mysticism advocates "the annihilation of the selfhood" *(bittul ha-yesh)* in an attempt to reach a mystical union. The goal is to overcome the limitations of one's finitude in order to see only the divine light into which one is totally absorbed.

Judaism has had a long tradition of mysticism. Most scholars trace its origin to the early rabbinic period. The overall term for the movement, especially in the form it took in the twelfth century and beyond, is Kabbalah, a word meaning "reception" or "tradition." In essence it refers to the esoteric teachings of Judaism as they developed through the creativity and practice of the sages of the past.

The classic mystical text in Judaism is the *Zohar* ("The Book of Splendor"), which was composed in the late twelfth century by Moses ben Shem Tov de Leon in Guadalajara, close to Madrid, but attributed to a second-century rabbinic sage Rabbi Shimon ben Yohai. In the following two centuries, various teachers of mysticism wrote elaborate essays on the subject, and the movement established itself in all its splendor in Safed, in the Galilee region of modern Israel. Here, in what some refer to as the post-classical period, the teachings of Rabbi Isaac Luria (1534–1572) became paramount. The Ha-ari ("The Lion"), as he was called, wrote almost nothing but taught a great deal and, in fact, set up a novel school of mystical teaching. His students recorded his message in great detail. He had a short life (he was thirty-eight when he died), but it was one of deep contemplation. It is said that he led an often solitary life as a young man, frequently visiting a small island close to Cairo, where he lived, for long periods of prayer and meditation.

Rabbi Luria formulated a new theory of the creation, based on the sequence of some dramatic events. It began with the contraction of God *(tzimtzum)*. This made room for the existence of the universe. Some vessels sheltered the lights that emanated from the Divine, but they were unable to sustain the power of the light and therefore shattered *(shevirat ha-kelim)*. Luria's theory holds the ultimate hope that there will be a "mending of the universe" *(tikkun olam)*. Prayer, along with good deeds, plays a great role in this process, according to Luria's teaching. However, prayer, he added, is more than a simple expression of the heart. Its primary goal is *devekut*, by which he meant a mystical connection with God that brings ecstasy to the human soul.

This idea of ecstasy and joy became the cornerstone of Hasidism in eighteenth-century Poland, where it was established as a powerful movement by Israel ben Eliezer, the famous Baal Shem Tov. The BESHT, as he was called for short, wanted to give his contemporaries, especially those who were not so learned in Torah, a voice and an opportunity to worship God with their total being. He said, "The Divine Presence does not hover over gloom but over joy in the commandments."[14] He further maintained that God is found not only through the mind but also through the heart, and argued that communion with God is even more important than the study of holy books. And this had to be done by the individual alone. He taught,

> We say: "God of Abraham, God of Isaac, and God of Jacob," and not "God of Abraham, Isaac and Jacob," for Isaac and Jacob did not base their work on the searching and service of Abraham; they themselves searched for the unity of the Maker and his service.[15]

For these kinds of teachings, he was denounced as subversive by mainstream rabbinic Jews. They were afraid that he would undermine the prevalent custom of Torah study as the basis of Jewish life. Yet, the Baal Shem Tov's ideas took hold among his followers. Some Hasidic masters, such as Menahem Mendel of Vitebsk (1730–1788), went even further and advanced the extreme position that without such *devekut*, "all a man's Torah and all the precepts he carries out avail him nothing, God forbid."[16] His assumption is that man's basic humanity is found in his ability to be attached to something greater than he. In his discussion of the meaning of *devekut*, Menahem Mendel quotes the Baal Shem Tov:

> When two pieces of silver are to be soldered together, it is only possible to do so after the silver itself has been scraped clean at the place where they are to be joined, if the join is to take adequately. If there is tarnish or any other dividing matter on the silver, the join is bound to be ineffective.... A man must first scrape away something

of his self so that there is no tarnish nor anything else to act as a partition. Then can *devekut* be achieved.[17]

Most of the masters of Kabbalah preferred to speak of *devekut* as a spiritual communion with God, that is, establishing contact with the Divine, rather than a mystic union in which a person becomes totally lost in the embrace of God.[18] The purpose of Creation, they insisted, is to provide opportunities to achieve communion with God.

Other Hasidic masters, such as Rabbi Nachman of Breslov (1772–1811), spoke of *hitbodedut* (Hebrew for "being alone" [with God]) as a means of achieving communion with God. According to Rabbi Nachman,

> To be in solitude is a supreme advantage and the most important ideal. This means that a person sets aside at least an hour or more during which he is alone in a room or in the field, so that he can converse with the Maker in secret, entreating and pleading in many ways, of grace and supplication, begging God to bring him near to His service in truth.[19]

To make this communication personal and immediate, as the basis of individual spirituality for all times, he taught, "this prayer and supplication should be in the vernacular, namely, in these lands, German (i.e., Yiddish)."[20]

IN MODERN TIMES

In more recent times, the modern Hebrew terms *ruhaniyut* (or simply *ruhanut*), and more recently *penimiyut* ("inwardness") have been used by many Jewish thinkers to refer to what is commonly called spirituality. The intention of this spirituality is to sustain, strengthen, and nourish the nonphysical aspects of life as well as to foster a deeper appreciation for our existence as God's creation.

To the extent that these terms imply a certain distinction between body and soul/mind, they are out of line with contemporary thought. Today, body and spirit are considered inseparable. We don't really know where the body ends and where the soul/mind/spirit begins. They are all intertwined, and they work together. Matter turns to energy; energy becomes matter. Spiritual life, therefore, requires an integrated approach, one that addresses the needs of the whole person—body and mind together. Thus, Tamar Frankiel and Judy Greenfeld, experts on the mind/body/soul connection and its relation to Jewish tradition, note in their book *Minding the Temple of the Soul: Balancing Body, Mind, and Spirit through Traditional Jewish Prayer, Movement, and Meditation,* "Body, mind, and soul are interactive and interdependent forces or vital energies. Each has its own purpose and contribution to our lives…our approach to physical health must involve the spirit, and our approach to spiritual growth must address the body."[21]

Since biblical times, in considering the concept of God and the road to spirituality, many Jewish thinkers have developed a variety of theologies compatible with the premise that God is "one" (better, "unique"). The process continues even today. Among the new approaches are the following:[22]

- The existentialism of Martin Buber, where God is experienced as another but can only be met in an I-Thou setting of mutual affirmation.

- The religious naturalism of Rabbi Mordecai M. Kaplan and Roland B. Gittelsohn, who maintained that God is not a person but a Power or Energy within the universe that assists in our self-realization.

- The predicate theology of Rabbi Harold M. Schulweis, who understands God in terms of the moral quality of divine attributes.

- The limited theism of Rabbi Milton Steinberg and Rabbi Harold S. Kushner, for whom God has limited power but is still all good.

- The religious humanism of Erich Fromm, who argues that God is the image of one's higher self.

- The hylo-theism of Alvin J. Reines, who defines God as "the enduring possibility of being."

We view the word *God* through the prism of our idea of the Divine. Each of these God concepts, as well as others, opens a different approach to life. We each have a different frame of orientation as we confront our daily challenges, but it is ultimately the God idea we cherish that gives us our outlook on life. Our concept of God propels us to move forward with trust in ourselves and confidence in the world around us.

One of the by-products of our belief in a particular God concept is a personal spirituality that can be put to practice in different ways. Just as Judaism accepts a variety of God concepts, so does it allow its practitioners to identify a particular spiritual path for personal growth. In the next chapters, we study in detail those spiritual paths within Judaism that to me represent the most significant among many alternatives.

CHAPTER 3

Spirituality through Acts of Transcendence

Now Moses, tending the flock of his father-in-law Jethro,
the priest of Midian, drove the flock into the wilderness,
and came to Horeb, the mountain of God. An angel of
the Lord appeared to him in a blazing fire out of a bush.
He gazed, and there was a bush all aflame, yet the bush
was not consumed.

—Exodus 3:1–2

THE MOMENT OF DISCOVERY

ARCHIMEDES (C. 298–212 B.C.E.) WAS ONE of the greatest mathematicians in ancient Sicily. He invented several machines and formulated new theorems in geometry and calculus, including Archimedes' principle, which states that any object that floats on or is submerged in water is buoyed up by a force equal to the weight of the misplaced water. According to a popular story, he was in his bathtub when he made this momentous discovery. Overwhelmed by this experience, he ran naked through the streets, crying, "Eureka," namely, "I have found it."

In the realm of physics, many laws were discovered in similar fashion by careful observers and often by chance. For example, Sir Isaac Newton (1642–1727), an English scientist who formulated a theory of gravitation, recalled that the idea came to him while he was drinking tea in his garden and saw an apple fall. However, there are certain significant events in one's life that can be understood only in the context of a spiritual vocabulary. However brief, these instances compel us to confront the transcendent, namely, God. They give the individual a new insight, a novel perspective. In popular parlance, it is as if we had seen the light. And the result is usually the same: elation, exhilaration, personal metamorphosis, and action.

It is not always easy to determine the difference between these moments of transcendence and other paths of spirituality. It is a matter of degree:

- In most cases, these special events tend to be intense peak experiences occurring on rare occasions.

- They often come up unexpectedly and then remain in the background as a remembered beacon of light.

- They frequently create a new pattern of life for the individual, a new style of living.

- They cannot always be duplicated.

People who have had such an experience will say that their lives have been changed forever. And in the majority of cases, they function under the new insight for the rest of their lives.

Today, social scientists know of the transformational character of these events in the life of individuals. These days we see such dramatic examples among the so-called *hoz're bit'shuvah* ("those who return [to religion] in repentance"). Often, a dramatic occurrence in their life leads irreligious or antireligious people to repudiate their past and to become very observant in an effort to mend their ways. Similarly, for many Jews a trip to Israel is more than a casual travel experience. It is a pilgrimage. For centuries, Jews have prayed for a return to the land of their ancestors; touching the stones of the Western Wall is an over-whelming religious experience that has transformed many people into lovers of Zion.

WHAT JEWISH TRADITION TEACHES US

The Hebrew Bible contains other examples of these kinds of tran-scendent experiences.

We are told that while tending his father-in-law's flock in Midian, Moses saw a bush flaming without being consumed. When God began to speak with him, he, startled by the experi-ence, realized the importance of the moment and instinctively "hid his face, for he was afraid to look at God" (Exodus 3:6). Similarly, our ancestor Jacob, on waking up from a dream in Bethel, proclaimed, "How awesome is this place! This is none other than the abode of God, and this is the gateway to heaven" (Genesis 28:17). In these examples, both Moses and Jacob expe-rienced something extraordinary that transformed their lives. They felt exposed to the overwhelming "Presence of God."

In the religious life of the biblical Israelites, the concept of the Presence of God plays an important role. An understanding of this idea opens for us a new perspective on their spiritual quest. During their peregrinations through the desert, we are told, the ancient Israelites often experienced the *kevod YHVH* (Exodus 16:7, 16:18, 24:17; Leviticus 9:6, 23, etc). This Hebrew expression, usu-ally translated as "the glory of the Lord," is a technical term in the Bible. The basic meaning of *kavod* comes from the Hebrew root *KVD* and implies "heaviness," "weight," and therefore "honor." Referring to God, it encompasses the multifaceted aspects of the divine image reflected in the Hebrew Bible. In some biblical texts, this *kavod* is manifested in a storm (Psalms 29:3; 19:1). On other occasions, it appears as fire and a rainbow "which shines in the clouds on a day of rain" (Ezekiel 1:28). According to Exodus 16:10 and Leviticus 17:7, the "*kevod YHVH* appeared in the cloud." During the revelation on Mount Sinai, this *kevod YHVH* looked like "a devouring fire on top of the mountain in the sight of the people of Israel" (Exodus 24:17). In some biblical texts, God's *kavod* is said to fill the whole creation. In a well-known passage in the Book of Isaiah, the prophet relates that he had "seen" the Lord in the Temple seated on a throne and surrounded by angelic beings that declared: "Holy, holy, holy! The Lord of Hosts, His Presence *(kevodo)* fills all the earth" (Isaiah 6:3).

God's *kavod* can also be perceived in historical acts. Here is a good example: "I will stiffen Pharaoh's heart," says God to Moses, "and he will pursue them [i.e., the Israelites], that I may gain glory *[Ve-ikkavedah]* through Pharaoh and all his host; and the Egyptians shall know that I am the Lord" (Exodus 14:4; Ezekiel 28:22).

By studying all the usages of this expression in the Hebrew Bible, especially in the priestly writings, it becomes apparent that there is a close connection between God's *kavod* and the cultic experiences of the ancient Israelites. On the basis of this observation, some scholars have argued that some Temple objects, such as a lamp, a flame, or incense, must have represented this Presence.[1]

In the medieval period, the concept of God's *kavod* received special attention among Jewish philosophers. In particular, Moses Maimonides made it very clear that "the glory that is spoken here is His essence,"[2] which can be seen only through an "intellectual apprehension" and in no way does this refer to the vision of a human eye."[3]

God's *kavod* also refers to divine attributes. A good example of this particular meaning can be found in a remarkable passage in Exodus 33. After the episode of the Golden Calf, Moses asks God to let him see the divine *kavod*.

> He said: "Oh, let me behold Your Presence *(kevodekha)*!" And
> He answered: "I will make all My goodness *(tuvi)* pass before

you, and I will proclaim before you the name Lord, and the
grace that I grant and the compassion that I show." "But," He
said, "you cannot see Me and live." And the Lord said, "See,
there is a place near Me. Station yourself on the rock and, as
My Presence *(kevodi)* passes by, I will put you in a cleft of the
rock and shield you with My hand until I have passed by. Then
I will take My hand away and you will see My back; but My
face must not be seen. (Exodus 33:18–23)

In other words, according to biblical teaching, no human
being can ever see God's Presence.[4] At Horeb/Sinai, we are told,
the Israelites heard the "voice" of God but saw no form
(Deuteronomy 4:12, 15–18). Even Moses, who "knew" God "face
to face" (Deuteronomy 34:10), is given the privilege of "seeing"
only God's back.[5]

People still experience God's commanding Presence or Glory
by observing supernatural phenomena, and are awed by its
grandeur. Others "see" the acts of God in the workings of history
or in a conflation of events that radically change their lives or give
them a tremendous elation. Many people find this sort of divine
encounter in the miracle of birth. Each of these represents a precious spiritual experience that enriches the individual emotionally and intellectually, and fills him or her with a sense of great
awe.

EXAMPLES FROM THE PAST

Nathan of Gaza (1643/4–1680)

In Jewish history we have records about many individuals who
underwent profound turnarounds in their personal life after experiencing a transcendent moment. Frequently the result is a
move toward Judaism, but at times it is away from it. One such
dramatic case of spiritual renewal occurred in the life of Nathan

of Gaza, who was one of the most important figures of the Sabbatean movement in the sixteenth-century Ottoman Empire.[6]

Born in Jerusalem in 1643/4 as Abraham Nathan ben Elisha Hayyim Ashkenazi, he received an intensive rabbinic education from some of the best teachers of his time. At an early age, he developed an interest in mysticism and studied Kabbalah. In the early months of 1665, he had a vision of how the world was created—a scheme that differed in many respects from that of Rabbi Luria.

During the same year, in mid-May, when Sabbetay Zevi, the charismatic Kabbalistic teacher of Smirna (now Izmir, in modern Turkey), arrived in Gaza, Nathan's transcendent moment occurred. He fell into a trance and announced Sabbetay's new role as the long-awaited messiah before the assembly of rabbis.

Sabbetay, who had come to have his soul repaired by Nathan, now found himself in a totally different position. On May 31, in Gaza, at the instigation of Nathan, Sabbetay Zevi formally proclaimed himself messiah and quickly swept along with him the entire community, including its well-known rabbi, Jacob Najara. Nathan assumed the role of "the prophet of the son of David" and became Zevi's foremost interpreter and spokesperson.

This endorsement gave Sabbetay Zevi the needed impetus to spread his message throughout the Mediterranean basin and beyond. Thousands and thousands of Jews followed him. Through various letters, publications, and decrees, Nathan formulated rules of penance called *tikkunim* ("mendings") for all the increasing number of believers of the newly established messianic movement. He was highly successful and remained so for a long time, even after the apostasy of Sabbetay Zevi to Islam in 1666. Nathan continued to preach that the messiah, Sabbetay Zevi, would return in God's own time. After wandering around through Thrace and Greece, he died in Skopje in 1680. His grave remained a pilgrimage site for many generations until World War II, when it was destroyed.

Franz Rosenzweig (1886–1929)

The German Jewish philosopher Franz Rosenzweig had a religious experience on the eve of Yom Kippur that transformed his life forever.

Born in Kassel, Rosenzweig grew up in an assimilated Jewish family. They de-emphasized their Jewishness, mainly because of their fear of anti-Semitism. The Rosenzweigs had incorporated the values of the surrounding German culture and considered themselves to be basically German. When Franz entered the university in 1905, he pursued studies in philosophy, history, and classics. During those school years, many of his relatives and friends formally converted to Christianity on the basis that they had already accepted the Christian culture as their own. At any rate, they were Jewish only in name. Converting to Christianity did not represent a major change in their lives.

When pressure was placed on Rosenzweig to follow their example, he refused to do so because he believed that conversion was a cowardly act. Later on, while in Leipzig in 1912, he ran into one of his relatives, Eugen Rosenstock-Huessy, who was on his way to become a major Protestant theologian. Eugen urged Franz either to defend his limited Jewishness or to come out with courage and convert to Christianity. After intensive thought, Franz decided to convert, but he stated that he would do so not "as a pagan" but "as a Jew," in the manner of the early Christians who had grown up in the Jewish community.

He was prepared to carry out his decision after the High Holy Days in 1913. That year, he had the opportunity to attend services in a small Orthodox synagogue in Berlin. This experience had a major impact on him. He never recorded what transpired in his own soul that special day, but something of tremendous importance must have occurred. The emotional high of the Yom Kippur service transformed him into a believing Jew as well as a committed one. Instead of going to the baptismal font, he came out of the experience reversing his decision. In fact, he chose to spend the rest of his life explaining his own roots and the meaning of being a Jew. He resolved to recover Judaism not only for himself but for others of his generation as well.

Martin Buber (1878–1965)

The Jewish philosopher Martin Buber, who maintained that "All real living is meeting,"[7] taught that there are two kind of relationships: I-It and I-Thou.

I-It is a relationship of use and experiencing, such as when one summons a cab to go from point A to point B. Here one relates to the other from object to object. There is no mutuality here. On the other hand, in the I-Thou relationship, one relates to the other from subject to subject. There is mutuality and confirmation of selves. Even though the I-Thou contact is a passing one, there is, Buber believed, a Thou, which by its very nature cannot become an It. And that is God, the "Eternal Thou."

Buber relates how he was transformed by this recognition when a seemingly everyday event happened to him:

> When I was eleven years of age, spending the summer on my grandfather's estate, I used, as often as I could do it unobserved, to steal into the stable and gently stroke the neck of my darling, a broad dapple-gray horse. It was not a casual delight but a great, certainly friendly, but also deeply stirring happening. I must say that what I experienced in touch with the animal was the Other, the immense otherness of the Other, which, however, did not remain strange like the otherness of the ox and the ram, but rather let me draw near and touch it. When I stroked the mighty mane, sometimes marvelously smooth-combed, at other times just as astonishingly wild, and felt the life beneath my hand, it was as though the element of vitality itself bordered on my skin, something that

was not I, was certainly not akin to me, palpably the other, not just another, really the Other itself; and yet it let me approach, confided itself to me, placed itself elementally in the real relation of Thou and Thou with me. The horse, even when I had not begun by pouring oats for him in the manger, very gently raised his massive head, ears flicking, then snorted quietly, as a conspirator gives a signal to be recognizable only for his fellow-conspirator; and I was approved.[8]

CONTEMPORARY EXPERIENCES

Transcendent experiences occur to almost all of us, but few of us take note of them. However, when we do, we realize that they are transformative in nature and have deep spiritual overtones. Let me share a personal story:

In 1961, I was in Babaeski, Thrace, a small village not too far from the Greek border, serving as an officer in the Turkish army's tank corps. At the time, this was a sensitive area of Turkey, and people were in a state of high alert. One night I was on patrol duty. It was standard procedure then to issue separate passwords for each night. Both soldiers and supervisors were privy to this "secret" information. As you approached the special observation post, the soldier would say: "Stop; what is the password?" You would respond by uttering the code word. If correct, then the soldier would allow you to approach him. If there was a discrepancy, he had the right to shoot you on the spot.

That night the code word was issued to all of us, and at midnight, I began to make the rounds as the officer in charge. One after another I checked key points in the military compound, was properly acknowledged, and gave the necessary instructions to the soldiers. Finally I decided to check a secluded hill where I knew I had placed a young cadet. As I approached the location he stopped me and asked for my password. I blurted it out, but to my surprise, bewilderment, and shock, he told me it was wrong.

I immediately realized that I was in danger. Obviously, the soldier had forgotten or misunderstood the code word and was expecting a different one. I tried to make myself visible by coming into the moonlight. But he must have misinterpreted my move as an evasive tactic, for he immediately raised his rifle and took aim at me. For a moment my entire life flashed before my eyes. I could not believe that I could be dead right there and then because of the foolishness of this person who had the wrong information. I remembered a rabbinic teaching that I had heard in my religious school: "Repent one day before your death, for you do not know when is your last day on the face of the earth" (Av. 2:10; Avot de Rabbi Natan, 15). All the knowledge I had acquired, all the skills I had mastered, all the values I cherished, all the relationships I had established were about to come to a tragic end at any moment. I thought I needed to do something—and something fast. I started to talk to him in a loud voice, hoping he would recognize me in spite of the darkness of the night. Something must have clicked, for he slowly lowered his rifle and in a friendly tone asked me, "Is that you, Lieutenant Rifat?" "Yes," I replied with great relief, "it is me." "Oh," he said, "I am sorry, I did not recognize you." At that point, I did not know whether to reprimand him or express gratitude to God for sparing my life in the middle of a lonely hilltop.

This experience had a profound influence on me and on my view of life and of God. Later, as I pondered the implications of this event, I realized I had gained, in those few moments, a recognition that our life is ephemeral. We come and go like grass that shoots up in the morning renewed, and then in the evening fades and withers (Psalms 90:5–6). We have limited control over our life; at times, it is snatched away by pure coincidence or a tragic event. I therefore developed a greater appreciation for life itself as a gift from God that must be acknowledged with gratitude. It is remarkable how a single event in one's life can generate so much feeling and be the source of a powerful spiritual encounter with the Highest we know.

IN NATURE

Nature often plays a great role in fostering acts of transcendence. As Ellen Bernstein, the founder of a Jewish environmental group called Shomrei Adamah (The Keepers of the Earth) and editor of the first major work in the emerging field of religion and the environment, remarks, "When you ask someone where they have experienced the presence of God, they invariably say on a mountain top or by water, rarely in a modern synagogue."[9] Here is her story:

> Late one afternoon, having spent the entire day climbing, we reached a summit ridge. As evening descended, the three of us walked silently on a gentle trail, each absorbed in our own thoughts. I had been hiking for at least ten hours but wasn't tired. Even with a fifty-pound pack, my steps were light and effortless. I was mesmerized by the panorama of oceanic mountains that surrounded me and propelled by the rhythm of my feet touching the ground. The soft golden light of the setting sun cast the forest in an emerald glow. I was captivated by the moment and felt lifted and humbled. Every breath inspired me. I had discovered the meaning of worship.[10]

IN LIFE CYCLE EVENTS

A transformative moment of high spiritual content may also occur during a peak life-cycle event. Tirzah Firestone, rabbi and author, tells us about such a moment during the birth of her daughter. Here are her words:

> When the moment of delivery finally came and the doctor laid my baby on my chest for the first time, I exploded with emotion.... Up until Emily arrived, the word *Shechinah* had been only a concept to me, used loosely to signify the feminine face

of God. Now the *Shechinah* became real, an everyday presence from which I was separate, but in which I seemed to be living, like a diaphanous state of consciousness that enveloped me. I knew something had changed for me as a result of the new experience I was having: For the first time in my life, I knew without any question that I was loved and that I was meant to be alive, doing exactly what I was doing at each moment. My normal state of mind—rushing, judging, comparing myself and my situation to an ever-rising standard—was now gone, leaving in its place a more contented state of being, with softer edges and a more compassionate heart. The new consciousness had everything to do with the baby I had been gifted with—she had opened me to it, as I had opened myself to her—yet it was not dependent upon her, but upon a divine force that was making itself known to me more clearly than ever.[11]

IN ORDINARY EVENTS

Transcendent moments can also happen during ordinary events in life and these infuse additional spiritual energies in us. Here is an example from Rabbi Terry A. Bookman of Temple Beth Am in Miami, Florida:

Had I been asked, twenty years ago, to write this piece, "What constitutes the spiritual in your life?" I might have talked about prayer, nature, being alone. Yet, without a doubt, the two most spiritual undertakings of my life have been the births and raising of our children and the work I have done as a rabbi of a suburban congregation. Then, I thought, I had to get away to seek the spiritual. Today, I understand more and more that changing a baby's diaper in the middle of the night, playing football catch with my son after a killer day at the temple, lifting the phone to say, "Mazal Tov," or, "Thank you for the program," or, "I'm sorry for your loss"—these are the exchanges which help to constitute the steps along my spiritual path.[12]

DURING RITUALS

Religious ritual frequently creates an appropriate context for transcendent moments. Here are two examples.

Ina Glasberg, a past president of my synagogue and a national member of the UAHC board, relates the following:

> Each year, during the chanting of the Kol Nidre, along with other officers of the Temple, I have the privilege of holding a Torah on the pulpit. I am usually given the "Holocaust Torah" due to its being smaller in size and lighter in weight. For the past ten years I have cherished this act while listening to the Cantor and the choir sing this most spiritual hymn in the liturgy of the High Holy Days.
>
> Last year something unusual happened that is difficult for me to explain or describe. The Torah was placed in my arms. The chanting of the Cantor began. Her lovely voice and the choir's response lifted our spirits to newer heights. I had the Torah on my left side, close to my heart. Suddenly, I felt my heart beat as if it were the heartbeat of the Torah itself. My eyes filled with tears. I was choked with emotions. This overwhelming sensation was indescribable.
>
> When I returned to my seat, I was drained. I reflected upon the meaning of such a strong heartbeat. Was I truly feeling the beat of the Torah—which is the heart of our people—or was I thinking of all those who had given their lives so that we would have the opportunity to pray together in freedom? Maybe both. But whatever the reason—and I am still pondering the question—the emotion I felt that night will stay with me forever.[13]

Rabbi David A. Cooper, a pioneer in Jewish meditation, relates such an experience when he entered the *mikvah* (ritual bath) in Jerusalem:

> The pool was all mine. I had waited a long time in the shower, peeking around the corner, hoping for a few moments of solitude. This was my reward: I was alone. As I hastened into the steaming tub, I pulled out the large rubber stopper in the wall that connected this water with an unseen source. The inflowing stream was cool. As the waters mixed, my tub was spiritually impregnated and validated as an authentic *mikvah*. Somewhere within my being, I felt a charge when this coupling occurred. I was secure, encased in a womb, warm, wet, and peaceful. Spreading my arms, I floated a few moments, supported, caressed, gently rocked in the spiritual amniotic fluid, lulled by whispering steam leaking through exposed pipes near the ceiling....
>
> I was curled near the bottom of the pool. The tugging became insistent. Slowly, I found the tiled bottom and pushed myself upward. As I broke through the surface into the world of mundane reality, I gently allowed my lungs to fill with the pervasive damp, warm air, and I knew something had been revitalized within me. In this daily experience of Jewish baptism was an affirmation and direct realization of a Kabbalistic secret: We are reborn each day—indeed each moment—and we begin afresh with the possibility of new perfection in every breath we draw.[14]

WITHIN THE COMMUNITY

In Judaism, community plays a great role in developing a Jewish identity. At times, the realization that one is a part of *Klal Yisrael* ("the community of Israel") can be transformative. Here is an example by Beth Moskowitz, a prominent lay leader in the Conservative movement in the greater Boston area:

> The Unity Mission I attended a number of years ago was a transforming event. The Unity Mission is a unique program here in the Boston area, sponsored by the Synagogue Council of Massachusetts. Leaders from Orthodox, Conservative, Reform, and Reconstructionist congregations join together as a group and travel together to New York City to study, pray, and have discussions with those from the other Jewish denominations.... It was this experience of *Klal Yisrael* that began my transformation of who I am today as a Jew.[15]

AS GOD'S PARTNER

As we have seen, these transformational experiences often cause a dramatic change in one's life pattern. Linda Sacks, a physician, tells of how the impact of such a spiritual moment can give a person new insight into his or her work.

> As a neonatologist, I care for critically ill infants in Savannah, Georgia's sole neonatal intensive care unit. Erin, whose parents were members of my *shul*, was born twelve weeks before term.

> As Erin lay hovering between life and death, our rabbi stopped by to fulfill the *mitzvah* of *Bikur Cholim*, visiting the sick. It was his first visit to neonatal. Two-pound Erin, struggling for every breath, lay under a radiant warmer connected to intravenous lines, chest tubes, and noisy machines.

> Standing at her bedside, our Rabbi quietly opined: "This unit is truly *tikkun olam*. You are finishing God's work."

A chill passed through me. Although I took pride in my profession, I never dared think of my medical role as a partnership with God. That profound realization forever changed my relationship with my tiny patients and their parents.

I began to see ill neonates, not just as other cases to be cured, but as incomplete human beings with yet unrealized potential. I began to relate to the suffering of their families in a more empathetic light. It is now infinitely easier for me to spend hours at a bedside fighting to keep a preemie alive, knowing I am doing God's work rather than just practicing medical science, earning a living, and avoiding malpractice suits.[16]

WITNESSING A MIRACLE

There are also those who are spiritually energized by amazing events in their lives that border on the miraculous. For example, Rabbi Daniel B. Syme, of Temple Beth El in Bloomfield, Michigan, notes that

While biblical miracles are told and retold today, most often as legendary tales, the modern mind finds it difficult to accept the notion of miracles. I do not share that cynicism, for in my lifetime I have been part of moments that, for me at least, transcend any scientific explanation.... There have been moments in my life in which I have known God, situations in which I have felt a sense of God's presence so deeply that I gave voice to the certainty it gave me without doubt and without the slightest hesitation. Why then? Why me? I do not know, but I will retain absolute belief in the possibility of miracles until the day I die.[17]

FINDING MOMENTS OF TRANSCENDENCE— RISING TO THE OCCASION

There are moments in life that call for an extra special effort. They call us to rise to the occasion. These too can be transcendent experiences that take us outside of ourselves. They propel an individual into a new role and create memories worthy of praise. Some people are willing participants and are ready for the occasion. Others are pushed higher and accept the challenge only with reluctance, if not fear.

Examples are plentiful: the substitute teacher who is called on to take over the class because of the main teacher's maternity leave; the assistant conductor who is asked to lead the orchestra upon the sudden death of the old maestro; the newly ordained minister who arrives to a new pulpit only to find out that the next day he or she needs to conduct a funeral in a tragic case. Many of us have been pressed into such a service at one time or another. Sometimes we do an adequate job, but sometimes we rise to the occasion and surpass everyone's expectations, including our own. At those moments we feel an exhilaration that is often spiritual and transcendental. During those moments, many feel the Presence of God: We are not alone; we have truly surpassed ourselves.

In the Biblical period, many of the prophets recorded for posterity what they considered to be significant "calls" by God to carry out a specific task. Amos tells us that God simply "took him from following the flock" and told him to "Go, prophesy to my people Israel" (7:15). Similarly, Jeremiah describes his childhood experience when "The Lord put out his hand and touched my mouth, and the Lord said to me: Herewith I put my words in your mouth" (1:9). Ezekiel's "call" is more elaborate. He received from God's hand a scroll "inscribed on both the front and the back; on it were written lamentations, dirges, and woes" (2:10), and he devoured it at God's command (3:2). These prophets accepted their new role with reluctance. So did Moses, who cried in dismay, "Please, O Lord, I have never been a man of words" (Exodus 4:10). He had to be convinced that he was the right person for the job. The prophet Isaiah, too, was forced into accepting his commission after one of the angels flew over with a live coal and singed his lips (6:6–7).

Once they accepted their task, these prophets and others like them carried out their duties with total dedication. They saw themselves as divine messengers. As Dr. Sheldon Blank, my Bible teacher at Hebrew Union College–Jewish Institute of Religion, noted, there is ample evidence that "the prophet regarded himself as a passive instrument by whom—one might almost say "by which"—God spoke."[18] Their words were God's words, which Ezekiel tells us "tasted as sweet as honey" (3:3) and were, therefore, compelling as well as irresistible. That is why they spoke without fear and with full confidence in their mission.

We are not prophets. In fact, even the ancient rabbis agreed that the era of prophecy had come to an end long before. Yet, the divine word continues to be spoken through sages and wise leaders. Though some believe that the Sinai revelation belongs to the past, and all we have to do is study, analyze, and interpret its message, others forcefully argue that the word of God can be heard even in our own time and that divine revelation is ongoing, is progressive, is a perennial occurrence. Rabbi Meir ibn Gabbai, a sixteenth-century Kabbalist originally from Spain, seems to endorse this concept when he writes,

> The true source from which the Torah and the Oral Law emanated never desists, it flows everlastingly…. The great voice never pauses, forever calling in its eternity, and all the prophets and sages in every generation have ever taught, conceived or decided, came to them from that perpetual voice containing all rulings, decrees and instructions, as well as all that will ever be conceived in the future.[19]

This idea was reflected in the Columbus Platform of Reform Judaism of 1937, which emphasized, "Revelation is a continuous process, confined to no one group and to no one age."[20]

The question of discerning the true word of God, or the word worthy of divine attribution, is a difficult and a sensitive one. Many pretend to speak in the name of God, including the murderous "Son of Sam" and Yigal Amir, who assassinated Yitzhak Rabin in November 1995. Yet, most people are likely to give credence to the message if it comes to heal, not kill; to build, not tear down; to pursue justice and peace, not foment discord and trouble; to bring wholeness, not break people and things apart. An act or a speech that uplifts the soul and directs it toward the betterment of society may be worthy of carrying the rubric "divine."

ACTS OF TRANSCENDENCE AS A PATH TO SPIRITUALITY

That these acts of transcendence have transformational power are documented in many sources. The moment itself may be unique, but the result is definitely long lasting. Buber teaches us that I-Thous do not last long. As soon as we become aware of them, judgment interferes, and quickly turns them into I-Its, the normal relationships of use among human beings. Even his own I-Thou meeting with his horse, which we read of earlier, came to an end. Writes Buber,

> Suddenly I became conscious of my hand. The game went on as before, but something had changed; it was no longer the same thing. And the next day, after giving him a rich feed, when I stroked my friend's head, he did not raise his head. A few years later, when I thought back to the incident, I no longer supposed that the animal had noticed my defection. But at the time I considered myself judged.[21]

According to Buber, a genuine meeting with God ends in personal enrichment. We return to our work with a greater insight and with deeper sensitivity. "Meeting with God," he writes, "does not come to man in order that he may concern himself with God, but in order that he may confirm that there is meaning in the world. All revelation is summons and sending...[for] he who goes on a mission has always God before him."[22]

Many of us who have had such unique spiritual moments in our lives feel tremendously enriched by them. For those who have not yet been blessed with this kind of an experience, this spiritual path is open if only we keep our eyes open, know how to seize the transcendent moment, and recognize it for what it is: a spiritual height of profound impact.

CHAPTER 4

Spirituality through Study

God said to David: "I prefer one day you spend in Torah
study to a thousand offerings Solomon will bring on the
altar."

—Sab. 30a

MOST PEOPLE WHO ENGAGE in study simply seek to acquire a
skill or collect information. But there are some who can
reach higher. For them study is a way to attain insight and illu-
mination. By delving into the intricacies of an ancient or a modern passage, people can and do use this learning method to uplift
their soul. They quickly discover that the text before them yields
new understanding of ethical and religious values. When they are
fortunate enough to come up with an insight about themselves
or the world around them, including what God stands for, they
feel as if they are transported to a loftier sphere that imparts profound meaning and purpose to their existence. For students of
Torah, this is the highest level possible. It is an ecstatic, emotional, and spiritual experience. Torah study for them is "an elixir
of life" (Ta. 7a).

THE WORD *TORAH*

The Hebrew term *torah* is a rich cultural word with multiple layers of meanings. Coming from the root *YRH*, it basically denotes

"to throw," "to direct," "to point the way," and therefore, "to instruct". In general, it stands for (divine) instruction and guidance. Much wider and deeper than its regular rendering as (divine) Law, it encompasses not only the entire corpus of biblical and rabbinic legal tradition but also all the moral teachings and religious doctrines attributed to God and the rabbis, past and present.

In actuality, the expression *Torah* (without the definite article) has a much wider connotation than "the Torah." Basically, the Torah is a scroll, a book, a sacred document, a particular teaching, which has a beginning and an end, as seen in the formula pronounced by Ashkenazic Jews during the raising of the Torah scroll: "This is the Torah *(ha-torah)* which Moses placed before the children of Israel, issued from the mouth of God through the mediation of Moses." On the other hand, the word *Torah* by itself represents all of Jewish wisdom through the ages, from the beginning to now. This Torah is not complete. It is interpreted and re-created at every generation by insightful sages.

In the early texts, the word *Torah* occurs in connection with the oracular use of the Urim and Thumim, the sacred lots cast by the priestly Levites (Deuteronomy 33:8–11). Although Torah was not the exclusive domain of the priests, they seem to have had a special responsibility for it (Leviticus 10:11; Deuteronomy 33:10; Jeremiah 2:8; 18:18; Hosea 4:6). During the monarchy, the term progressively assumed a wider meaning and included instruction provided by YHVH, such as certain specific laws: "Torah of the meal offering" (Leviticus 6:7); "Torah of the Nazirite" (Numbers 6:21).

In the post-exilic period, Torah covered the basic substance of the five books now attributed to Moses (Nehemiah 8:8; Ezra 3:2). By the second century B.C.E., the Torah referred to the Pentateuch, as distinguished from the Prophets and other sacred books. Later on it meant the entire TaNaKh, a word made of the initials of the three parts of the Hebrew Bible as we know it today: Torah, Nevi'im (Prophets), and Ketuvim (Writings). In the rabbinic period, the term *Torah* was applied to both the written Torah *(torah she-bikhtav)* and the oral Torah *(torah she-be' al pe)*, which, according to tradition, were received together on Mt. Sinai (Av.1: 1). Ultimately, *Torah* came to refer to the entire corpus of traditional texts.

WHAT JEWISH TRADITION TEACHES US

According to the teachings of Simon the Just, one of the sages who lived in the third century B.C.E., Torah constitutes the first of the three foundations of civilization, the other two being worship *(avodah)* and carrying out deeds of lovingkindness *(gemilut hasadim)* (Av. 1:2). Here the word *torah*, as most commentators note, most likely refers to *talmud torah*, the study of Torah. The term *avodah* is a technical term, which describes the sacrificial service carried out by the priests during the Temple period. Later on, it meant worship in general. The third element, *gemilut hasadim*, is wider than almsgiving and includes compassionate personal service of all kinds.[1]

In biblical times, the responsibility to impart Torah was primarily in the hands of the priests. We read: "You [i.e., Aaron] must teach *(u-l'horot)* the Israelites all the laws which the Lord has imparted to them through Moses" (Leviticus 10:11; Deuteronomy 24:8–9, 31:11–12, 33:10, etc.). These instructions seem to be basically directed to the laws connected with cult and ritual. In addition to the priests, prophets too are known as imparters of Torah (e.g., Isaiah 1:10; Zechariah 7:12). Torah was also taught by parents (Deuteronomy 6:6) and by the sages, *hakhamim* in Hebrew. Their teachings included not only advice and commandments but also words of Torah (e.g., Proverbs 4:2, 13:14). In Jeremiah 8:8 they even appear as legal scholars.[2]

In Jewish life, it is a *mitzvah* (an obligation) and a praiseworthy act to study Torah. "Happy is the person," writes the Psalmist, in whom "the teaching of the Lord *(torat YHVH)* is his delight, and he studies that teaching day and night" (1:2). "Train yourself to study Torah, for the knowledge of it is not inherited" urged Rabbi Yossei (Av. 2:17). According to the *Sefer Hahinukh*, the Book of Education attributed to an anonymous scholar in thirteenth-century Spain, "It is a positive precept *(mitzvat 'aseh)* to learn the wisdom of the Torah and teach it: in other words, how we are to carry out the precepts and keep away from what God has forbidden us; and likewise to know the ordinances of the Torah in accord with the truth."[3]

The centrality of *talmud torah* has remained constant throughout the centuries and was recently reaffirmed in the "Statement of Principles for Reform Judaism" approved by the Central Conference of American Rabbis (Reform) in May 1999. It reads: "We are called by Torah to lifelong study in the home, in the synagogue and in every place where Jews gather to learn and teach."

The obligation to study and teach has always been emphasized by generations of rabbis and community leaders. Joshua ben Perahyah (second century B.C.E.) taught, "Get yourself a teacher and a fellow student with whom to study (Av. 1:6; see also 1:16). Shammai, a rabbi of the first century C.E., urged everyone to make the study of Torah a fixed habit (see Av. 1:15).

The responsibility of Torah study is placed on every individual, regardless of background. Moses Maimonides clearly states, "Every Jew, whether poor or rich, healthy or sick, young or old and feeble, is required to study Torah" (*Mishneh Torah* 1:8). "If he has an important business to transact," states the Code of Jewish Law *(Kitzur Shulchan Arukh)*, "he should first study at least one verse of the Torah or one law, then attend to his affairs and thereafter complete his regular assignment" (I/27:1). "If someone was not taught by his fathers who have this duty," adds the *Sefer*

Hahinukh, "such as his father and his father's father, he is oblig-
ated to teach himself when he is grown and become aware of the
matter.... Until when is every man duty-bound to study Torah?
Till the day of his death."4

The pursuit of Torah study being a high priority in Jewish life,
many ancient rabbis have left us records of their own practice in
this area. We read, for example,

> It is said of Rabban Yohanan ben Zakkai that during his en-
> tire life he never used profane speech, nor walked four cubits
> without studying Torah or without wearing tefillin; nor did any
> man arrive earlier than he at the house of study, nor did he
> sleep or even doze while there; nor, when he went out, did he
> leave anyone in the house of study; nor when he happened
> to be in a filthy alleyway did he meditate [on sacred subjects];
> nor did anyone ever find him sitting silent—he was always en-
> gaged in study. (Suk. 28a; *Legends,* 210)5

Similarly,

> Rabbi Eleazar said: Never in my life has anyone preceded me
> into the house of study, nor have I departed from it leaving
> anyone there. (S. of S. R. 1:1, #9; *Legends,* 411)

The ancient rabbis preferred that Torah study be done within
a group or with another companion. Thus did Rabbi Hananya,
the son of Teradion, teach in the Mishnah,

> When two sit together and words of Torah are spoken
> between them, the Divine Presence *[Shechinah]* rests with
> them. (Av. 3:3)

However, Torah study is so important that with divine blessing it can be done even alone. The same rabbi continues,

> Whence do we learn that even if one sits by himself and en-
> gages in Torah study, that God appoints him a reward?

Because it is written [in Lamentations 3:28], "Let him sit alone in silence, since He has laid it [i.e., Torah study] upon him."(Av. 3:3)

In the past, the obligation to study and teach Torah was placed solely upon men. Again, the *Sefer Hahinukh* says, "A woman has no obligation to teach her son [Torah]: for whoever is not under the obligation to learn is not under the obligation to teach."[6] Yet, it adds, "It is right for every woman to endeavor that her sons should not be ignoramuses, even though she is not commanded by the law of the Torah; and good reward will be hers for her effort. So too, if a woman studies Torah there is reward for her."[7]

In our time, both men and women are encouraged to study and teach Torah. And many do, from elementary schools to universities and rabbinic and cantorial schools. In some very traditional synagogues, girls receive Jewish education separately from boys. As of today, no Orthodox Jewish women are ordained as rabbis or invested as cantors, even though there are many women teachers who teach Torah at almost every level of the educational structures within the Orthodox Jewish community. On the other hand, liberal Jews have had coeducation in their respective religious institutions for decades. Consequently, they have men and women functioning as rabbis, cantors, and educators in congregations as well as in universities, including rabbinic and cantorial schools as well as schools of education.

STUDY VERSUS PRACTICE

Rabbis have discussed the relative value of study. What is more important, they asked: to know or to act? The majority of the sages seem to have placed practice above study. "The purpose of learning," states Rava, "is repentance and good deeds" (Ber. 17a). Practice is preferable, teaches Rabbi Tarfon (Kid. 40b). Another rabbi, Rabbi Hiyya, goes even further when he states that "He who studies without intending to practice, it were better if he had not been created" (Lev. R. 35:7).

The sages of the rabbinic period were academicians with a good practical mind. They knew that some people engaged in Torah study "as a crown with which to magnify themselves or as a spade to hoe with" (Av. 4:5; Ned. 62a)—in other words, to derive personal benefit from it. But they also hoped that many among them, through the proper discipline of study, could elevate themselves into leading a life suffused by the values of Torah. Therefore, they stressed that "Your study should lead to practice" (Av. 6:5), for "not the expounding of the Torah is the chief thing, but its practice" (Av. 1:17, 3:13). Rabbi Akiba believed that study indeed comes first, for in the end it leads to correct observance (Kid. 40b).

According to our sages, the study of Torah requires individual discipline and, at times, even personal sacrifices. Thus, for example, we read,

> This is the way of Torah: you shall consume a morsel of bread with salt, you shall drink a measure of water, you shall sleep on the floor, and live a life of hardship, as you engage in Torah. But if you do this, "happy you shall you be, and it will be well with you" (Psalms 128:2). (Av. 6:4)

On the other hand, the ancient rabbis tell us that the study of Torah brings with it many benefits. For example, Torah teaches gentle manners (Pes. R. 17b). It is the source of decent human relations (Av. 3:21). It restores one's spirit (S. of S. R. 1:2). It is equivalent to offering a sacrifice and therefore atones for our sins (Men. 11a; Tanh. B., Ahare Mot 35a). It relieves one of "the yoke of government and the yoke of worldly concerns" (Av. 3:5). Its rewards are endless, reads one text: "As the words of the Torah have no limits, so does their reward" (Pes. K. 107a).

According to a talmudic sage, Rabbi Phineas ben Jair, *talmud torah* has other dividends. It "leads to precision, precision leads to zeal, zeal leads to cleanliness, cleanliness leads to restraint, restraint leads to purity, purity leads to holiness, holiness leads to meekness, meekness leads to fear of sin, fear of sin leads to saintliness, saintliness leads to the [possession] of the holy spirit, the holy spirit leads to life eternal" (Avoda Zara 20b, Soncino). The author of *Sefer Hahinukh* states the purpose of this endeavor as follows: "The root reason for this precept is known [obvious]: for by learning, a man will know the ways of the Eternal Lord (be He blessed), while without it he will neither know nor understand, and will be reckoned as an animal."[8]

TORAH FOR ITS OWN SAKE

It appears clear from these statements that for many of the ancient sages, Torah study must have some practical results. Torah must be translated into good deeds. However, ancient rabbis were also aware of the long tradition in Jewish life of studying Torah for its own sake. They called this *torah lishmah* and placed a high value on it. Thus, Rabbi Eleazar ben Rabbi Zadok taught, "Speak words of Torah for their own sake" (Ned. 62a). Similarly, commenting on the Biblical passage "She opens her mouth with wisdom, and the torah of lovingkindness is on her tongue"(Proverbs 31:26), Rabbi Eleazar asked,

> Is there one Torah of lovingkindness and another Torah not of lovingkindness? [The answer is this:] It means that the Torah studied for its own sake is, in fact, a Torah of lovingkindness, while the Torah not studied for its own sake [namely, for an ulterior motive] is a Torah not of lovingkindness. (Suk. 49b; *Legends*, 414)

Similarly,

We have been taught that Rabbi Banaah used to say: "He who occupies himself with Torah for its own sake—the Torah he masters becomes an elixir of life for him. But he who occupies himself with Torah not for its own sake—the Torah becomes for him a deadly poison." (Ta. 7a; *Legends*, 414)

In order to highlight the benefits of *torah lishmah,* many sages drew attention to the numerous personal rewards that one can receive from pure intellectual stimulation. They maintained that study itself not only increases one's knowledge about God and the Jewish way of life but also contains certain hidden blessings in personal growth. Rabbi Meir, for example, listed some benefits that accrue to a person who engages in Torah study for its own sake:

If you study Torah in order to learn *[lishmah]* and do God's will, you will acquire many merits; and not only that, but the whole world is indebted to you. You will be cherished as a friend, a lover of God and of people. It clothes you with humility and reverence; it enables you to become righteous and saintly, upright and faithful. It keeps you far from sin, and brings you near to virtue. You benefit humanity with counsel and knowledge, wisdom and strength. It gives you a commanding personality and an ability to judge. Its secrets are revealed to you. You become like a gushing fountain, like a never-failing river. You are modest, slow to anger, and forgiving of insults; and it magnifies and exalts you above all things. (Av. 6: 1; *Guide of the Perplexed,* 27)

Another sage, Rabbi Alexandri, taught that the person who studies Torah for its own sake becomes an instrument of peace: he "makes peace in the household above as well as the household below" (San. 99b). Rabbi Levi argued that this individual also brings the redemption near (idem).

Yet, it must be recognized that study for study's sake is not easy. In fact, it requires a discipline that many people sorely lack. Most people expect that the time spent in probing a particular text will have immediate relevance to their daily life and yield concrete results. Aware of this individual need, many ancient rabbis encouraged people to engage in Torah study even if it was done for practical reasons at the beginning. As Rabbi Judah taught in the name of Rav: "A person should occupy himself with Torah study even if it is not done for its own sake, for as he busies himself not for its own sake, he will end up occupying himself with it for its own sake" (Naz. 23b). Or, as we read elsewhere, "Study out of love, and honor will come in the end" (Ned. 62a). These sages knew the difference between getting information and obtaining an education, and they were willing to train their students so that they would ultimately appreciate learning for its own sake.

TORAH STUDY AS A PATH TO SPIRITUALITY

We human beings are blessed with an inquisitive mind. We must start with "I don't know" and seek answers regarding our existential condition. "Without knowledge," says an ancient sage, "how can there be discernment?" (J. Ber. 5:2). The answer is this: the more we study, the more we acquire the skills that will enable us to understand ourselves, the world around us, and God, who makes it all possible.

The prophet Jeremiah taught that if a wise person has to boast at all, let him at least boast that "he has the wisdom to know Me [God]," for this is what God wants (Jeremiah 9:23). Commenting on this verse, the philosopher Moses Maimonides takes this idea even further and argues that the ultimate purpose of human life and activity is to "know" God. Toward the end of his *Guide,* he writes,

> The perfection of which one should be proud and that one should desire is knowledge of Him, may He be exalted, which is the true science.[9]

But what does it mean to "know" God? In the Bible, Isaiah complains that the people of Israel does not recognize God's supreme authority:

An ox knows its owner,

An ass its master's crib;

Israel does not know (yada)

My people takes no thought.

(1: 2)

As Dr. Sheldon Blank (z"l), my Bible teacher at Hebrew Union College–Jewish Institute of Religion, remarked, God "demands da'at, 'knowledge of Him,' and knowledge of him meant not only awareness of his true nature and demands but also, and more significantly, acknowledgment or acceptance by his people of his authority."[10] For the prophet Jeremiah, knowledge of God meant doing deeds of kindness:

He judged the cause of the poor and needy; then it was well.

Is not this to know me?

Says the Lord.

(22:16, RSV)

Similarly, the prophet Hosea states,

For I [God] desire steadfast love and not sacrifice, the knowledge of God, rather than burnt offerings. (6:6, RSV)

For Maimonides, "knowing God" has more of a philosophical meaning, which has to do with the human mind attempting to reach the Divine. He says that even when Jeremiah argues, in 9:23, that an individual should boast only when he "knows" God, this means "he should glory in the apprehension of Myself and in the knowledge of My attributes, by which he [Jeremiah] means His actions."[11] He writes,

> In this verse [v. 23], he [Jeremiah] makes it clear to us that those actions that ought to be known and imitated are lovingkindness, judgment, and righteousness…. It is clear that the perfection of man that may truly be glorified in is the one acquired by him who has achieved, in a measure corresponding to his capacity, apprehension of Him, may He be exalted, and who knows His providence extending over His creatures as manifested in the act of bringing them into being and in their governance as it is.[12]

Yet, even Maimonides admitted that not every person is willing to accomplish all that, or capable of it. Only the rarest of human beings—such as the prophets—can achieve this lofty goal. For, as he noted elsewhere,

> One should know that among men are found certain people so gifted and perfected that they can receive pure intellectual form. Their human intellect clings to the Active Intellect, whither it is gloriously raised. These men are the prophets. (Helek: Sanhedrin, Chapter Ten, Sixth Fundamental Principle)[13]

How do we accomplish the task of *talmud torah?* Rabbi David Wolpe, of the University of Judaism in Los Angeles, writes,

> Jewish study is supposed to bring the student closer to God. That is why study is often conducted aloud, in a singsong chant. It is more than an intellectual operation; it is a way of arching one's soul up toward the divine and finding God inside oneself.[14]

Talmud torah is a powerful means to appropriate the Sinai experience of our ancestors. As Susie Schneider, a meditation teacher in Jerusalem, remarks,

The Light accessed through text study provides us with the
pure light of Sinai, undiluted and unattenuated. It is a thick,
sweet, blissful light that fills our soul, our heart, and our bones.
The text of the Torah itself as well as all of the writings that it
has spawned has this power to link back to the fire of Sinai.[15]

By engaging in Torah study, we see ourselves in the light of the
text. It quickly becomes not someone else's story but our own. We
see our own reflection in it and are also illuminated by it, both as
individuals and as members of the community. As Dr. Carol Ochs,
coordinator of the graduate studies program at Hebrew Union
College–Jewish Institute of Religion, and Rabbi Kerry M. Olitzky,
of the Jewish Outreach Institute in New York, write,

Through study...the text of our lives has become the sacred
text of our people's journey through history as they struggled
in relationship with the holy. We use our own experience as a
prism to understand what the Bible is teaching us. At the
same time, we use the Bible to illuminate our experiences. As
a result, we see things, both in the text and in our lives, that
we might not otherwise have seen.[16]

Torah study is a major ingredient of personal spirituality. In the
words of Rabbi Lawrence Kushner, an author of many books on
spirituality and mysticism, "Study is a meditative and transformative act.[17] It nourishes our soul, gives us direction in life, and sharp-
ens our mind. The sacred text, elucidated by past generations and
students of our time, becomes a road map for us as we face daily
challenges. It provides us with the means to make responsible moral
decisions. It elevates our spirits and helps us enter into a dialogue
with the Divine in life. In the words of Rabbi David Hartman, the
founder and director of the Shalom Hartman Institute of Jerusalem,
"The student experiences the presence of God even in those aspects of Torah created through human interpretation."[18] No wonder we are enjoined to recite a prayer before *talmud torah* by
saying, "Praised are you, O God, who has sanctified us with

mitzvot and instructed us to engage in matters of Torah."

But Torah study cannot be productive if it is not done on a regular basis. It is a lifelong discipline. The Bible reminds us, "Let not this Book of the Teaching *(sefer ha-torah)* cease from your lips, but recite it day and night" (Joshua 1:8). In Pirke Avot, we read, "Make the study of Torah a fixed engagement (1:15; see also Erub. 54b). "The path of learning," notes Rabbi David A. Cooper, Director of the Heart of Stillness Retreat Center in Boulder, Colorado, "is the process of refining our awareness by dedicating time each day to the study of uplifting material. When we read inspirational books, our hearts soften. This path of practice, however, requires more than an occasional book. Rather, it requires that we assume the habit of daily study and thereby continuously add spiritual and mystical sweetener to our lives.[19] (See also Av. 1:15.)

CONTEMPORARY EXPERIENCES

Numerous individuals have indicated their preference for this spiritual dimension of Torah study over other types of spirituality. Their words and examples provide us with different perspectives.

Rabbi Norman J. Cohen, provost and professor of midrash at Hebrew Union College–Jewish Institute of Religion, and author of *The Way Into Torah*, writes,

> I remember the first paper that Rabbi Borowitz assigned to us in the introductory course in modern Jewish philosophy/theology. It was entitled, "How Do I Experience God's Presence?" After struggling with the topic for some time and trying to characterize how I felt when I prayed and how (or even if) prayer helped me to sense God's presence, I realized that more than in any other context, it was in the exhilaration of studying Torah and trying to find personal meaning that I felt a true sense of both grounding and uplift at the very same time. For me, Talmud Torah is the path to sensing closeness with the divine, with feeling the *Shechinah*'s presence.[20]

Similarly, Rabbi A. Stanley Dreyfus, former director of rabbinic placement for the Reform movement, writes,

> I encounter spirituality not only when I join in the statutory services of the synagogue, but also when I work at construing a Hebrew text in my study.[21]

Francine Klagsbrun, a well-known Jewish writer and lecturer, states her position as follows:

> For me, the antidote to the excessive focus on spirituality— be it feminine or masculine—is a return to the serious study of texts, whether through adult education programs or study groups, university courses or private investigation. For in those texts—the Pentateuch, the Prophets, the Writings—lies the core of Jewish history and morality, of ethical views and social legislation. Sure, there are things to dislike in the texts, things to argue about and rant against. But first there must be study, and from study knowledge. Remarkably, some will find, study itself can lead to transcendence, and knowledge can be the source of the highest spirituality.[22]

Similar opinions are expressed by Michael J. Bohnen, a prominent attorney and community leader in Boston:

> While I have personally witnessed many miracles firsthand, those were not necessarily my most spiritual moments. I have attended the births of my children (among my happiest moments), and I have seen sickness healed. I was in Israel to see with my own eyes the prophesied return to Zion of the remnants of my people from Ethiopia and Russia. I can sense Heschel's "radical amazement" when I take the time to see nature's wonders, large and small. I believe in the power of prayer and respond especially strongly to the liturgy of the awesome day of Yom Kippur.

While these are all powerful moments of awareness, wonder, and appreciation, none approaches the sense of engagement with the Divine that I have when I study the Torah, written and oral. My earliest memories of this sort are discussions I had as a child with my father about the weekly Torah portion as we walked to *shul* together on Saturday mornings. Now I have this experience when I attend a weekly *shiur,* a Talmud class, where, under the guidance of an expert, we study the search for God's will as articulated in the debates of the sages of the Mishnah and Gemara, in the explications of Rashi, in the dialectics of the Tosafists, and in the pronouncements of Maimonides. It is a stimulating intellectual exercise, but it is much more than that. There is a sense of delving into the Divine Plan.

When I first studied the midrash that refers to the Torah as God's "blueprint" for the universe (Ber. R. 1:1), it struck a very responsive chord. It is our access to that blueprint that can transform the text into a road map for a profoundly spiritual journey. We can aspire to walk in God's way and, as it were, think God's thoughts. The text, which we hold sacred, provides us with an inspired view of our world and its history, and an inspiring set of guidelines for interpersonal behavior and interaction with God.

Like the Moliere character, the bourgeois gentleman, who was astonished to learn that he had been speaking "prose" for over forty years without knowing it, it took some time before I recognized the strong spirituality inherent in the study of sacred texts.[23]

In Jewish life, *talmud torah* rarely exists in a vacuum. Very often, prayer and other types of spiritual paths accompany it. Study leads to knowledge, knowledge raises the sense of wonder, and this sense of awe is the basic ingredient of prayer, which for some is a prominent gateway to spirituality.

CHAPTER 5

Spirituality through Prayer

Out of the depths I have called to you, O God.
—Psalms 130:1

F OR MANY INDIVIDUALS, engaging in regular prayer is a major
part of their spirituality. Prayer time is sacred time to com-
municate directly with the Divine in an intimate way. At the end
of worship, the pray-er leaves with a sense of contentment and
wholeness.

THE ESSENCE OF PRAYER IN JEWISH TRADITION

In English, the verb *to pray* is a transitive verb, derived from Latin
and Old French, meaning "to obtain by begging" or "to entreat."
In Hebrew, the most common word for prayer is *tefillah*.[1] It comes
from the verb *lehitpallel*, a reflexive form of the root *pll*, which
means "to judge." Therefore, at the very basic level, *to pray* really
means "to judge oneself." When Jews engage in prayer, they look
into themselves as they try to relate to the Source of all Existence:
God.

Human beings have prayed since the beginning of time. They
have opened their hearts to God in times of trouble as well as joy.
We have records of such prayers going all the way back to the
Sumerians, who inhabited the ancient Near East as early as 4500

B.C.E.[2] The Hebrew Bible contains many prayers uttered by individuals.[3] Unlike the prayers of other religions of the ancient Near East, prayers in the Bible are directed only to God, not to other presumed intermediaries.

During the First Temple period, the primary means of communal worship was a sacrifice, brought in for a variety of reasons. It is not clear whether or not prayers accompanied these offerings. Though the Bible contains a few personal prayers (e.g., Numbers 12:13; Exodus 18:10; I Samuel 1:11), most scholars argue that, especially during the pre-Exilic period, worship took place in silence, with priests reciting some formulas. Most of the action was on the altar. During the Second Temple period, the pattern appears to have changed. With the creation of the *maamadot* system, whereby some community representatives were present at the Temple sacrifices while the rest of the people assembled in a home to recite some prayers, formal community liturgy started to emerge. The Book of Psalms, most of which comes from the post-Exilic period, contains a number of prayers stressing praise, gratitude, and petition. Our present prayer structure comes primarily from the ancient rabbis who created many of our private and communal prayers that exist in our prayer books.[4]

A prayer is an attempt to connect with God. It is a bridge between a person and the Divine. In the words of Rabbi Harold Kushner, a prominent author of many books on modern Jewish thought, it is "the experience of being in the presence of God."[5] During prayer, the individual who offers up the thoughts of his or her heart is able to connect—not always, but occasionally— the inner self with the Source of all life. For, as Rabbi Burt Jacobson of Kehilla Community Synagogue in Berkeley, California, writes, "True prayer...is not just a turning inward. When we link ourselves with our own centers, with the Seed of Light within us, we simultaneously link ourselves with the One Center, the hidden Hub around which the whole universe turns."[6]

THE NEED FOR PRAYER

Prayer comes out of a personal need to relate to someone infinitely greater than oneself. It gives praying individuals new insights and deeper understanding of themselves, and thus prepares them to face the world with courage and clarity of mind. Every prayer becomes a program of action, motivating them to accomplish their tasks with determination. Recently, healthcare professionals have demonstrated the benefit of using prayer before surgery and while patients are undergoing difficult treatments in order to improve their recovery times. Prayer has been shown to be of value for the overall well-being of stressed men, women, and even children.[7]

The need for prayer also emerges because people want to express their gratitude for the wonders they see in the universe. In fact, for the Jewish philosopher Abraham Joshua Heschel (1907–1972), this element is the fundamental component of any prayer. He writes, "To pray is to take notice of the wonder, to regain a sense of the mystery that animates all beings, the divine margin in all attainments."[8] Similarly, commenting on the biblical text "Let every breath praise the Lord" (Psalms 150:6), one ancient sage taught, "At each and every breath a person takes, he should praise his Creator" (Gen. R. 14:9; Deut. R. 2:37).

For Tamar Frankiel of the Claremont School of Theology, and Judy Greenfeld, a certified fitness trainer and founder of Homeaerobics, a prayer is a spiritual workout: "Prayer is really our way of singing ourselves into existence before God. The Talmud describes it as an *avodah,* as labor, service, or work: 'You shall serve the Lord your God with all your heart' (Deuteronomy 11:13). 'How does one serve with the heart? By praying' (Ta. 2a). But it is a different kind of work from our everyday occupations, since it is work on oneself, a kind of spiritual workout.... Prayer is a time of self-evaluation. Yet, it is above all a healing process, not a lecturing to ourselves. We chant, sing, and sway, using the words of inspired poetry handed down through the ages, in order to cleanse away the old and make way for the new. It is a work of using the mind to look into the heart, placing ourselves in a closer union with God; it is a time to become aware of love, awe, trust, and faith."[9]

Is there a distinction between worship and prayer? Rabbi Harold Kushner says yes. He writes, "Worship is any form of putting ourselves in contact with God—with the Spirit that guides us to human fulfillment. We may worship through study, through deeds of kindness and helpfulness, through an act of self-control, through charity, and we may worship in many other ways. Prayer is worship through the use of words."[10] The Israelites believed that God pays attention to prayers and petitions and thus could be addressed with confidence:

All mankind comes to You

You who hear prayer.

     (Psalms 63:3)

This assumption was based on historic experiences. As Dr. Moshe Greenberg, a biblical scholar and esteemed teacher, points out, "the capability of prayer arises out of a prior experience of God's turning to men."[11] This applies both to individuals and communal petitions.

Thus the patriarch Jacob prayed:

Deliver me, I pray, from the hand of my brother Esau; else, I fear, he may come and strike me down, mothers and children alike. Yet you have said, "I will deal bountifully with you and make your offspring as the sands of the sea, which are too numerous to count." (Genesis 32:11–13)

"Perception of such divine working, "adds Greenberg," is the life-breath of prayer, of petition and praise alike."[12]

TYPES OF PRAYER

Individuals pray under different conditions and on various occasions. In order to respond to different moods, our prayer books contain various types of prayers. Rabbi Louis Jacobs of the New London Synagogue, a prolific author, argues for four categories: petition, adoration, thanksgiving, and penitence.[13] Rabbi Milton Steinberg (1903–1950) adds contemplation, affirmation, resignation, protest, and quest to the list.[14] Dr. Carol Ochs and Rabbi Kerry M. Olitzky speak of the following types: petition, intercession, thanksgiving, confession, silent prayer, communal.[15]

Some biblical prayers are very short, like the one uttered by Moses when Miriam, his sister, became ill: "O God, pray heal her!" (Numbers 12:13). Others, such as King Hezekiah's prayer (II Kings 19:15–19), are much longer. Some prayers are expressed extemporaneously; others are recited from a written text. The ancient rabbis knew that there was a tension between these two forms. Ideally, every prayer should spring out of the heart at the time when the individual is ready for it. Thus, Rabbi Simon taught, "Do not make your prayer a routine but a plea for mercy, and a supplication before the Holy One" (Av. 2:13). However, this would make community worship impossible. People need a common text in order to share hopes and aspirations, especially when the prayers themselves are in a plural voice. Therefore, the rabbis made room for both forms of prayer, even within the same worship service. Thus, for example, in the *tefillah* (also called the *Amidah* ["standing," for it is recited while one is standing up] or the Eighteen Benedictions), which is recited three times a day, there is a middle section called *bakashot* ("petitions"). In the early Talmudic period, this portion had no set order. This freedom allowed the praying individuals to offer prayers as their heart prompted them (Meg. 17b). Presently, many services allow people to pray silently to accomplish the same purpose.

CONCENTRATION

An authentic prayer requires mental preparation and deep concentration. The Hebrew term for this is *kavanah*, meaning "intention" or "directing the heart (to God)." As Rabbi Lawrence A. Hoffman, professor of liturgy at Hebrew Union College–Jewish Institute of Religion and author of *The Way Into Jewish Prayer*, indicates,[16] ancient rabbis used this term to refer to "the spontaneous and creative" aspect of prayer, as opposed to *keva*, the fixed aspect of the service. The expression came to refer to the inner concentration needed during worship. In mystical literature, it expanded to the esoteric meaning of the texts. In fact, many different *kavanot* were created for this purpose. The most important, among Sefardic Jews, is the following one:

> With this, I do prepare my mouth to thank, praise, and glorify
> my Creator for the sake of the unification of the Holy One,
> Blessed be He, and His Shechinah by means of the hidden
> and concealed one, in the name of all Israel.

According to the Mishnah, "The pious people of old used to wait an hour before they said the *tefillah*, in order that they might direct their heart toward God" (Ber. 5:1). Maimonides makes it very clear when he states, "A prayer uttered without mental concentration is not a prayer" (*Mishneh Torah* 2:4). He adds, "The mind should be freed from all outside thoughts and the one who prays should realize that he is standing before God" (ibid., 2:16). This is the reason why Jewish law states that in order to recite the *tefillah*, one must be sober (cf. Ber. 5:1). Maimonides highlights the following: "People should not stand up to pray after indulging in jest, laughter, frivolity, idle talk, quarreling, or outburst of anger" (ibid., 2:18). His rationale is that these individuals have been distracted and cannot properly concentrate. From *Sefer Hasidim* (thirteenth century), we have this suggestion: Better a short prayer recited slowly than a long prayer uttered hurriedly and without devotion (cf. #839).

DIFFICULTIES WITH PRAYER

Some people find it very difficult to pray, for various reasons. One reason is that with the advance of science today, events that were formerly called "divine workings" in the world are now often explained through natural causes and not as intrusive "acts of God," and this makes prayer seem irrelevant. Also, people who are not familiar with Hebrew find the Hebrew prayers too baffling at times. For some, prayer is not seen as a priority in their lives or an overwhelming need. There are also individuals who are hung up on specific details, such as the language of liturgical texts (e.g., not gender sensitive, not inclusive language), or the format of the prayer service (e.g., repetitions, sitting and standing, bowing and kneeling), or the seating arrangement (e.g., mixed sitting versus separation of women and men), or the relevance of the music or the sermon, or even the environment in which communal prayer takes place (e.g., open air, too dark, sanctuary too large).

And there are those who are disappointed that their prayers go unanswered. This, of course, undercuts one of the basic rationales for petitionary prayers. However, this is not a new problem. Even in biblical times there were some who were disappointed with prayer. The Psalmist complained,

As for me, I cry out to You, O Lord;

each morning my prayer greets You.

Why, O Lord, do you reject me,

Do You hide Your face from me?

(Psalms 88:14–15)

Similarly, the prophet Habakkuk sobbed:

How long, O Lord, shall I cry out

And You do not listen.

(1:2)

Yet, in spite of this occasional divine silence, the biblical Israelite did not lose hope that in the end,

The Lord is near to all who call Him

to all who call Him with sincerity.

(Psalms 145:15)

In reality, the problem that many people have with prayer has little to do with prayer itself. Most of the issues just mentioned can be satisfactorily resolved once the underlying *raison d'être* of prayer is clarified, and that is the acknowledgment of one's own beliefs. Bluntly stated, to pray, one must believe. An authentic prayer depends on *how* one conceives of God. As Maimonides wrote, "True worship is possible only when correct notions of God have previously been conceived."[17] For Maimonides, the "correct" notion was the Aristotelian idea, which he modified in light of the Jewish belief in the creation of the universe "from nothing": that God is the "Unmoved Mover," the One who set the universe in motion at the beginning of time. Today, most people would agree that there are various concepts of God, each one authentic in itself. Nevertheless, I still maintain that prayer emerges out of a particular concept of God, and that, as Heschel insisted, "The issue of prayer is not prayer; the issue of the prayer is God. One cannot pray unless he has faith in his own ability to accost the infinite, merciful, eternal God."[18]

Consequently, given the fact that the role of prayer depends on an individual's concept of God, it becomes evident, for example, that those who espouse a theistic view of God as a "personal God" of infinite strength would consider prayer an actual dialogue with the divinity. On the other hand, for religious naturalists who think of God as a "power" or "energy," prayer is basically the ability to utter one's hopes and aspirations. They do not feel that an answer is necessary or required. As Rabbi Mordecai Kaplan (1881–1983), the founder of the Reconstructionist

Jewish movement, states, prayer is simply "the utterance of those thoughts that imply either the actual awareness of God, or the desire to attain such awareness."[19] Similarly, once a person subscribes to a particular concept of God, then specific issues of worship such as the appropriateness of liturgical texts, the format of the service, or the environment where prayer takes place can be dealt with more easily.

Others, however, claim that theology is at the end of the process of prayer, not at the beginning. In other words, prayer leads to prayer. Thus, Rabbi Eric H. Yoffie, the president of the Union of American Hebrew Congregations, argues that "theology emerges from successful prayer; it does not precede it. Almost a thousand years ago, Maimonides was asked how you teach children to pray. The way you teach them to pray, he said, was to pray with them. In other words, you do not begin by teaching them theological doctrines; you expose them to the liturgy, the chants, and the experience of community, and most of the time, this will give rise to some form of belief…. So to those who say: 'first theology, and then prayer,' I would respond: 'no, first prayer—and the theology will take care of itself.'"[20]

THE OUTCOME OF PRAYER

The ancient rabbis, who sincerely believed in the power of prayer and its ability to affect the outside world, pointed to a few caveats regarding the scope of prayer. Even though they lived at a time when belief in the miraculous was very popular, there were some, like Raba, who insisted that "one does not rely on miracles" (Pes. 64b). Furthermore, the sages identified a category of prayer that should not be used: "To cry over the past is to utter a vain prayer *(tefillat shav)*" (Ber. 9:3). For example, the text continues, "A person whose wife is pregnant should not say 'May it be Your will that my wife should have a boy.'" Such prayer is vain, because the sex of the child has already been determined at the time of conception, and no prayer will alter it. Similarly, the sages said, if a person is coming home from a journey and hears cries of distress in his town, he is not allowed to pray, "God grant that this may not be in my house" (idem). Such prayer, too, is vain, because if the fire is at his house, it is too late for any prayer. (Furthermore, one could add, this prayer is immoral, because it implies the hope that the conflagration is in someone else's house.) The rabbis also added that there is a time for a short prayer and a time for a longer one. As an example, they cite the case of the Israelites, who facing the Reed Sea before them and the Egyptians behind, began to cry out to God (see Exodus 14:10ff.). Rabbi Eliezer then taught,

> God said to Moses: "My children are in trouble; the sea shuts them off on one side, the enemy pursues them on the other, and you stand and make long prayers." And God said: "There is a time to lengthen prayer, and a time to shorten it."
> (Mek., Beshallah, 4)

What is the efficacy of prayer? As we have said, the expected outcome of prayer depends on the theological views held by the person praying. Some people believe that prayer actually alters the course of events. Among them, mystics, who assume that everything in the universe is interrelated, even maintain that prayers here below directly affect the heavens above. Rabbi Marcia Prager, a Reconstructionist rabbi who is much attuned to modern-day spirituality, says, "Through the practice of blessing we develop an ever deepening receptivity to the abundant love and joy flowing through Creation…. We come to feel the Presence of God move within us and through us. The result is bliss."[21]

Most religious naturalists and humanists, however, would deny this assumption on the basis of observable phenomena and experience, and argue that prayer has the capacity to change only the pray-er. As Rabbi Harold Kushner writes, "Only when we pray for a change within ourselves is it possible for our act of prayer to influence the results."[22] To quote the prayer book *Gates of Prayer*, "Who rise from prayer better persons, their prayer is answered."[23]

AS A PATH TO SPIRITUALITY

Those who use prayer as a dominant path of their spirituality find that preparation for prayer is paramount. Hayyim Halberstam (1793–1876), known also as the Hasidic Rebbe of Tsanz, once was asked by a follower: "'What does the Rabbi do before praying?' 'I pray,' was the reply, 'that I may be able to pray properly.'"[24]

Rabbi Sheldon Zimmerman, president of Hebrew Union College–Jewish Institute of Religion, prepares for prayer by voicing the following words:

A Prayer for Prayer

O My God

My soul's companion

My heart's precious friend

I turn to You.

I need to close out the noise

To rise above the noise

The noise that interrupts—

The noise that separates—

The noise that isolates.

I need to hear You again.

In the silence of my innermost being,

In the fragments of my yearned-for wholeness,

I hear whispers of Your presence—

Echoes of the past when You were with me

When I felt Your nearness

When together we walked—

When You held me close, embraced me in Your love,

Laughed with me in my joy.

I yearn to hear You again.

In your oneness, I find healing.

In the promise of Your love, I am soothed.

In Your wholeness, I too can become whole again.

Please listen to my call—

Help me find the words

Help me find the strength within

Help me shape my mouth, my voice, my heart

So that I can direct my spirit and thus find You in prayer

In words only my heart can speak

In songs only my soul can sing

Lifting my eyes and heart to You.

Adonai S'fatai Tiftach—open my lips, precious God,

So that I can speak with You again.[25]

Some argue that there is a difference between praying and davening (or davvening), a Yiddish word meaning "to recite prayers." For those who follow the second path, praying appears too formal, whereas davening includes an element of ecstasy. Rabbi Shoni Labowitz, of Temple Adath Or and co-director of Mayyim Chayyim in Davie, Florida, gives us an example:

> There are moments when I pray by heart, moments when I pray by mind, and moments when I pray by body—and glorious days when all three forms of prayer become one.... I recall one time when I sitting lotus-style in front of the ark, meditating. It was a divine experience. At the conclusion of the meditation I felt the need to open the *siddur* at random. The page fell to *Alenu,* the concluding prayer of traditional services. I then instinctively felt that my partner God was compatible with my method of prayer that day.[26]

Rabbi Gershon Winkler, director of the Walking Stick Foundation, a spiritual center in Cuba, New Mexico, also prefers to daven. He writes,

> I do davven. Just not that way. Just not from preheated liturgy, be it liturgy of the eleventh century or liturgy baked at a *kallah* in Philly.... The longer I lived in the woods, the more I became aware that I was still davvening. Only my davvening had taken a different form, or rather had transmuted from form altogether to experience. When I take solitary walks in the woods where I live—and I do this quite often—I almost always end up davvening. It starts out sometimes as a mundane conversation, with nothing or no one in particular, not the trees, not the rocks, not God, not even myself. I just talk about what's on my mind.... And as I do so, I become engaged in conver-

sation. Something or someone out there seems to be listening, and, by listening, responding…. When I look up into the
great Beyond, this is the sense I get when I do these raps,
the sense that I am not looking into Outer Space, but into
great big gigantic, warm, comfortable ear. More of a Cosmic
Ear. More like God's ear…. So I see davvening as an act of
talking to God so that we could better hear ourselves; crying
out to God our deepest yearnings and concerns, so that we
can become more conscious of them ourselves.[27]

Not everyone, however, davens. The prayer experience, one
of the most potent spiritual events in one's life, has a unique
meaning for others. Roland Gittelsohn, rabbi of Temple Israel in
Boston (d. 1995), was one of them. As an army chaplain during
World War II, he composed and recited several prayers that profoundly affected him and the worshipers who were present with
him. One event stood out in his memory:

It was the most excruciating moral dilemma of my life, one
which obsessed me by day and kept me awake a good part of
each night. Since my high school years I had been an absolute
pacifist, a conscientious objector to war. Now that rock-like
conviction was under assault. Its still-stubborn persistence was
augmented by a strong desire not to be separated from my wife
and two very young children. I rationalized, moreover, that especially at such a time of severe social crisis my civilian congregants needed me more than ever. On the other hand, we
were involved in a war, which might well determine the survival
of Judaism and the Jewish people. In addition, young men in
my congregation were being drafted; they did not enjoy my
luxury of voluntary choice. What did I owe them? I prayed then,
more frequently and probably more fervently than ever before.

Gradually, in those moments of prayer, I moved (or was
moved?) toward a solution. I heard no voices, saw no visions

or signs. But I began to feel a Presence in my life, a Force, a Power, a Thrust which I had recognized before as a cosmic quality but not felt so immediately within my own mind and heart. Slowly an understanding developed that my decision was related to the very purpose for which the human adventure on this planet had been initiated. The same Power that had infused cosmic reality with order, with purpose, with more sensitivity, was operating within my psyche. I was being tested as God's partner.

The same Spiritual Strength supported and sustained me nearly two years later as I trembled fearfully in my two Iwo Jima foxholes. Also as I conducted the Seder ceremonies aboard an attack transport ship, knowing that a few hours earlier my dearest loved ones had experienced the same rituals, voiced the same words ten thousand miles away.[28]

Rabbi Gittelsohn's comments can be best appreciated when viewed within the framework of his personal theology. He belonged to a group of religious thinkers who identify themselves as religious naturalists. In contrast, those who call themselves theists conceive of God as an all-powerful and all-good "Person" that affects the universe from the outside. This thinking, Gittelsohn argued, "grew out of primitive man's ability to think of abstract qualities and processes."[29] By contrast, religious naturalists speak of God both as "the power behind nature," namely, the "Force" responsible for the order, harmony, design, and plan of whatever exists, and the "moral Power" of the cosmos; in other words, the nonphysical aspect of existence, the ethical goal, the pattern of perfection toward which we ought to strive throughout our lives. Combining the two, Gittelsohn defined God as "the Soul of the universe"; that is, "the creative, spiritual seed of the universe—the Energy, the Power, the Direction, the Thrust out of which the universe has expanded, by which the universe is sustained, in which the universe and mind find their meaning."[30]

The use of distinct terminology—"person" versus "power"—is important for the understanding of this particular concept of God. Theists tend to believe in a God who is "compassionate and gracious, slow to anger and rich in steadfast kindness" (Exodus 34:6) and the sole Creator of the universe, who continues to affect it from without. On the other hand, religious naturalists like Gittelsohn argue that God is "the activating or energizing agent within nature, not external to nature."[31] In other words, "God is like the yeast that makes the dough rise into a loaf of bread."[32]

Religious naturalists, it should be stressed, are not pantheists like Spinoza who claim that God and nature are one and the same. They maintain that God is larger than nature and functions within it as the energizing power in both the physical and the spiritual realms of existence.

If God, as religious naturalists argue, is not a Person but a Power and consequently is not aware of our actions, why pray? Is it possible to "address" a force, even if it is the "Power" or "Energy" of the universe? Rabbi Gittelsohn responds:

1. Prayer is a magnified wish.
2. Prayer is "tuning in" on God.
3. Prayer is taking inventory of ourselves.
4. Prayer is any form of reading, thinking, or meditating which reminds us of God as the ethical Goal of our lives and as the Power which can help us toward that Goal, and which inspires us to cooperate in our conduct with that Power in order to come closer to the Goal.
5. Prayer is any intellectual, emotional, or esthetic experience which seeks or strengthens one's spiritual relationship with the universe.[33]

It is unimportant, a religious naturalist would say, whether God "hears" our prayers or not. It is, however, very important that we do express our wishes and hopes in our prayers, and then turn them into programs of action.

SILENT PRAYER

Rabbi Alan Lew, of Beth Shalom in San Francisco, writes: "It's important to understand the language and the structure of the Jewish prayer service, but I think the real spirituality of the service lies elsewhere—in the rhythm of the service, in the flow of gesture and sound, and in the silences between and behind the language."[34]

I would venture to say that for a prayer to become a means of entering a spiritual state, it does not even need to be uttered aloud. As we have already noted, often in our worship services we have an opportunity to pray silently. At times, even a ritual act that accompanies a set of prayers can be a significant transcendental act. What happened to Dr. Samuel Kunin, a physician and a *mohel,* is a good example. He writes,

> I arrived for the berit with much curiosity and with some trepidation, entering a home filled with silence. All the guests, as well as the couple with whom she, the mother of the baby, lived, were either hearing or speech impaired. Only the signer spoke to me during the entire encounter. I prepared the baby in the bedroom, explaining the process to the mother through the signer. We called in the *sandek* [the person who holds the baby during circumcision], *kvater,* and *kvaterin* ["godfather" and "godmother," respectively], and discussed their duties. We were now ready. What followed was one of the most gratifying experiences I have had as a *mohel.*
>
> We walked into the living room and I had everyone "say" *barukh habah* ["blessed is the one who came"]. Most did it by signing. Some, in almost unintelligible guttural sounds, uttered these words. The mother signed her prayer before circumcision. [The mother was a single mother.] I explained the meaning of the word *berit* and spoke of Noah, Abraham, and Zipporah, weaving the meaning of the covenant into the sto-

ries of these biblical personalities. The circumcision was performed, and the guests responded, "Amen." The service continued with the blessing over the wine and the naming of the child, always with the appropriate responses. The *berit* ended with everyone expressing a hearty *mazel tov.*

In many ways, this was one of the great spiritual experiences of my life. In the midst of that enraptured silence, in the attentiveness of all the people there, in the looks on their faces, in their perfect responses, I knew this was a very special moment for them as well as me. We all learned something, and I was left with a memory that will last forever. This was a precious moment of silent prayer.[35]

The power of silence as a context for prayer can be gleaned from a remarkable passage in the Book of Kings, chapter 19, at text very much reminiscent of Exodus 33, where Moses takes refuge in a cave wanting to behold the presence of God, only to be told that "you cannot see My face" (Exodus 33:20). Here the prophet Elijah, frightened by the death threats of the queen Jezebel, hides in a cave in the desert. The text then goes on:

"Come out," He [God] called, "and stand on the mountain before the Lord." And, lo, the Lord passed by. There was a great and mighty wind, splitting mountains and shattering rocks by the power of the Lord; but the Lord was not in the wind. After the wind—an earthquake; but the Lord was not in the earthquake. After the earthquake—fire; but the Lord was not in the fire. And after the fire, *kol demama daka,* a soft murmuring sound. When Elijah heard it, he wrapped his mantle about his face and went out and stood at the entrance of the cave. Then a voice addressed him: "Where are you, Elijah?"
(I Kings 19:11–12)

Whether we translate the Hebrew words as a "soft murmuring sound" (NJPS) or as a "sound of thin silence" (Gray[36]), or stay with the familiar "a still small voice," it is clear that Elijah had a spiritual moment. That it is possible to encounter God in the midst of silence is also made clear in a famous passage in the rabbinic literature, which describes the giving of the Torah in these words:

> When God gave the Torah, no bird sang or flew, no ox bel-
> lowed, the angels did not fly, the Seraphim ceased from say-
> ing, "holy, holy, holy," the sea was calm, no creature spoke,
> the world was silent and still, and the divine voice said: "I am
> the Lord your God." (Ex. R. Yitro, 29:9)

USING MUSIC IN PRAYER

Right after a Grateful Dead concert, Lubavitch Rabbi Yosef Langer declared that "the people that are attracted to the Dead are looking for spirituality."[37] There is no doubt that music has a tremendous impact on one's religious expression. Some people experience this heightened spirit in a secular concert, whether of classical or popular music. Others find it in a liturgical setting. Recently, recordings of Gregorian chant have gained a newfound popularity. Among the Mevlevis, the mystic swirling dervishes in central Anatolia, it is dance accompanied by intensive religious music that provides the means toward spirituality.

In terms of its emotional impact, there is a palpable difference between reading a prayer and singing a prayer. In our synagogues, when the cantor and the congregation sing the traditional prayers in one voice, there emerges an unusual closeness and emotional uplift among the worshipers. In Hasidic gatherings, joining in a *nigun* (melody) is a most effective way to establish a sense of community as well as collectively reach out to the Divine. I have witnessed this kind of religious ecstasy during national Jewish conferences where four or five thousand people were united in liturgical singing. It is uplifting. It is spiritual.

One service in my synagogue that I find extremely moving is the Neilah service at the end of the Yom Kippur day. By this time, we have been in the sanctuary almost a full day. Though most of us are tired and hungry, there is a tremendous sense of participation. People are reading the prayers with *kavanah*. The congregation is singing almost in unison. There is a spirit of togetherness and a heightened sense of spirituality. I think it is the music that brings all of us closer to one another.

At Congregation B'nai Jeshurun (BJ, for short) in the upper West Side of New York City, music plays a major role during worship services. It is more than singing together. It is a happening! Hundreds of people gather on Shabbat to celebrate with song and music. They have even cut a CD entitled "With Every Breath" that highlights the music of Shabbat at BJ. The senior rabbi, Rolando Matalon, describes the role of music in his synagogue as follows:

> Music is central at BJ. Like the congregation itself, BJ's music honors the past as it wrestles with the challenges of the future. Music at BJ has helped to open the hearts and minds of thousands of Jews to the beauty and continuing relevance of Jewish prayer and the Jewish tradition. At BJ music is a vehicle to deepen *kavanah.* It is also an avenue for Jews who are ignorant or estranged from tradition to enter and to embrace its depths and richness. BJ's music provides a way for all Jews—even those still learning synagogue skills—to enter and participate in the experience of meaningful prayer.[38]

Because music is so powerful, others are now progressively adopting this pattern. Torah and *haftarah* chanting, even in English, are becoming more popular among all denominations in American Jewry. According to a report in the *Utne Reader* (March/April 2000), Jewish liturgical folk music now includes a variety of styles, including Jewish bluegrass, Jewish country, Jewish reggae—even Jewish rap. More adults are learning "trope" [cantillation of Torah and *haftarah*] these days than ever before. In doing this, people seem to be following the biblical injunction "Sing unto the Lord a new song" (Psalms 98:1) and the old rabbinic teaching that says, "If your voice is pleasing and you are seated in the congregation, rise up and honor God with your voice" (Pes. R. 25:2; *Legends,* 522).

In attempts to connect with the Divine, when people engage in spontaneous prayer; regularly participate in congregational worship; devote time to religious music, dance, or contemplation; or follow a discipline of meditation, they soon realize that any and all of these activities end up being incredibly powerful experiences. Through prayer, they can unveil their hopes and aspirations, give voice to their needs, proclaim gratitude for what they have and are, and ultimately turn these into deeds capable of benefiting themselves and others. It's no wonder that so many give preference to this particular means of expressing their spirituality.

CHAPTER 6

Spirituality through Meditation

> Meditation is designed to give you direct access to the
> spiritual.
>
> —Avram Davis

O F ALL THE SPIRITUAL PATHS traveled by those who seek spiritual enlightenment, none is more popular than meditation, whether in Eastern countries, where it is almost equated with spirituality, or even now in the Western countries, where meditation is becoming widespread among people in all walks of life. Why such interest in meditation? And where does meditation fit within the structure of Judaism? We shall now explore these important matters.

MEDITATION IN JUDAISM

Meditation has been used as a means of reaching a heightened sense of spirituality since antiquity. The Bible records a few visionary experiences, though it is difficult to identify them as meditation. For example, the text tells us that the patriarch Isaac, before meeting with his future wife Rebekah, "went out *lasuah* in the field towards evening" (Genesis 24:63). The meaning of the verb *lasuah* is not clear. In fact, the New American Bible (1970) leaves the text blank: "One day toward the evening he went out...in the field." The New English Bible (1972) has this: "One evening when he had gone out into the open country hoping to meet them," with a note saying, "or, to relieve himself." Many translations render it as "meditate," others as "walking." The ancient rabbis understand it as praying.[1]

In the Bible, as we noted before, many claim to have seen God but no one provides a description of God. According to Exodus 24:11, Moses and a few elders "beheld *(va-yehezu)* God, and they ate and drank." The Psalmist expresses the hope that he will "behold *(hazitiha)* You [God] in the sanctuary" (63:3). Job, too, has a similar expectation: "I would behold *(ehezeh)* God while still in my flesh" (19:26). Isaiah tells us, "I beheld *(va-ereh)* my Lord seated on a high and lofty throne" (6:1). The prophet Ezekiel records a vision where he saw *(va-ereh)* "visions of God" that had "the semblance of a human form" in the sky (1:26), which he then identified as "the appearance of the semblance of the Presence of the Lord" (v. 28). The message of the Scripture seems to be that God cannot be described. Even Moses, who "knew" God "face to face" (Deuteronomy 34:10) is told that "you will see My back; but My face must not be seen"(Exodus 33:23). Whether these visions are the result of meditation or contemplation is not known.

In the post-biblical period, we have clearer accounts about meditative activities. Philo of Alexandria (20 B.C.E. to 50 C.E.) spoke of spiritual contemplation. For him, when a person prays, "the mind abandons body and sense perception and becomes absorbed in a form of intellectual prayer, which is wordless and unencumbered by petition."[2] Later on, some rabbinic teachers followed in his footsteps, and they encouraged others during worship to rise above the world below in order to face or visualize the *Shechinah* (the Divine Presence). As one sage put it, "He who prays should regard himself as if the *Shechinah* stands before him" (San. 22a).

The early rabbis knew of mystical speculation but did not give it an enthusiastic approval, for they were afraid it could lead people astray. In fact, they wrote that

Four people entered the *pardes* ["orchard," i.e., field of mys-
ticism].... Ben Azzai looked and died.... Ben Zoma looked
and became mad.... Aher [name given to Elisha ben Abuyah]
cut down the plants [i.e., he became estranged from Judaism].
Rabbi Akiba emerged in peace. (Hag. 14b)

Earlier Kabbalists concentrated on two types of meditative
activities:

• *Maaseh bereshit* (the Act of Creation) focused on the process
by which the universe is created and sustained by God.

• *Maase merkabah* (the Act of the Chariot) was based on the vision of the prophet Ezekiel (ch. 1 ff.), and centered on as-
cending the higher levels of reality until one reaches the
Throne of God. According to Gershom Scholem, the German
Israeli scholar who established mysticism as an academic discipline in Judaism, "Here the reference is to an actual vision
of the world of the chariot, which reveals itself before the eyes
of the visionary."[3]

Ancient rabbis were very concerned about the dangers of
meditation, and restricted its practice to those who were mature
and well versed in Torah study. For example, we read,

The "Act of Creation" may not be taught in the presence
of two people. The "Act of the Chariot" may not be taught
even to one person, unless he is a sage and can grasp
it on his own understanding. Whoever speculates upon
four things, a pity on him!... What is above (i.e., heaven),
what is below (i.e., earth), what is before (the creation
of the universe), and what is after (i.e., the end of days).
(Hag. 2:1)

Maimonides, in medieval times, justifies the prohibition by
saying,

Not every one has the breadth of intellect required for obtaining an accurate grasp of the meaning and interpretation
of all its contents. (*Mishneh Torah* 4:11)

Rabbi Aryeh Kaplan, one of the pioneers of modern Jewish
meditation techniques, maintains that in the early rabbinic period the *Amidah* was composed as a meditation prayer, which
could be read either as a mantra or as a prayer.[4] An ancient mystical text of the sixth century (?), the *Heikhalot Rabbati*, recommends the repetition of a particular name of God 112 times. The
Zohar, the classic Kabbalistic text attributed to Moses ben Shem
Tov de Leon (c. 1280), contains visualizations of God as a means
of meditation. With the development of Kabbalistic literature in
Judaism, meditation became more prominent. The term *hitbonenut* (literally, "knowing oneself"), which encompasses both
contemplation and meditation, began to appear for the first time.
In fact, unlike Christian mystics who differentiated between these
two, Kabbalists maintained that "contemplation was both the
concentrated delving to the depths of a particular subject in the
attempt to comprehend it from all its aspects, and also the ar-
resting of thought in order to remain on the subject."[5] This could
lead to the contemplation by the intellect of words, names, or
thoughts.

During the thirteenth century, Kabbalists conceived of meditation using the *sefirot*, the ten emanations that appeared at the
beginning of Creation and that still sustain the universe, as a
medium. These were viewed as intellectual lights, which could
be reached by different types of meditation. Abraham Abulafia
(1240–1291), a famous Kabbalist, developed a system of meditation based on the magical powers of the Hebrew letters. Joseph
Caro (1488–1575), a mystic and the author of the *Shulchan Arukh*,
the most comprehensive Code of Jewish law, made use of
Mishnaic verses for the same purpose. The Kabbalistic teacher
Moshe Cordovero (1522–1570) developed a complex technique

of using Bible verses as mantras. The rise of Hasidism in eigh-teenth-century Europe placed meditation among the most often observed religious duties. Many Hasidic leaders, such as Hayyim of Volozhin, Shenur Zalman of Lyady, Nachman of Breslov, often well versed in Lurianic teachings, became masters of Kabbalah, wrote commentaries on mystical texts, penned original writings on mysticism, and recommended different types of meditative techniques.

In our day, meditation is widely practiced by many Jews as a daily exercise. Numerous books and how-to manuals have re-cently been published, introducing the general public to this dis-cipline. Avram Davis, a respected teacher of Jewish meditation and founder of Chochmat Halev, a center for Jewish learning and meditation in Berkeley, California, even believes that "the current revival of Jewish meditation is one of the best opportu-nities for the spiritual survival of the Jewish people."[6] Nan Fink Gefen, a Jewish meditation teacher and author of an introduction to Jewish meditation, identifies three major sources of contem-porary Jewish meditation techniques: (1) the Jewish meditative tradition, (2) the creative work of meditation teachers today who use Jewish symbols and images, and (3) the influence of Buddhism today. She remarks that "almost a third of American Buddhists are Jewish by birth. Many of these people have found a spiritual path within Buddhism that they didn't find within Judaism, but they want to reconnect with their Jewish roots."[7] She does not seem to be bothered by this intrusion, for she adds, "We are pleased to introduce them [i.e, the seekers] to Jewish meditation. As they learn about it, they bring the knowledge and wisdom gained from Buddhism to their practices. Their insights help to shape the direction of Jewish meditation." In fact, there are those who, like Sylvia Boorstein, a teacher of mindfulness and a practicing psychotherapist, say that one can easily be "a faithful Jew and a passionate Buddhist."[8]

The underlying theological assumptions of modern Hasidic

and mystical teachings have to do with the belief that there is nothing but God whom, they insist, we recognize intuitively. God cannot be described or totally known. God is referred to as *En-Sof* ("without end"). It is not that everything is God—that would be pantheism—but that everything is in God ("panentheism"). Everything is suffused by God. As Rabbi Lawrence Kushner writes,

> Everything is organically joined to everything else. We have been players in a divine scheme, neither marionettes nor zombies but waves in a ocean, dancers in a ballet, colors on a canvas, words in a story. Discrete and probably autonomous, but never entirely independent.... Everything is *within* God.... The only thing truly within our power, and our power alone, may be whether or not we will behave in each moment with arrogance or reverence.[9]

This reverence is nothing but a sense of awe for the universe as a whole. Rabbi James L. Mirel of B'nai Torah in Bellevue, Washington, and Karen Bonnell Werth, a healthcare professional, write in *Stepping Stones to Jewish Spiritual Living,*

> In moments of deep meditation or expanded awareness, we may feel awe at the immensity of the universe—the beginning and the end of All Existence, the force of Creation and Transformation: God. Out of this consciousness come several ways of conceptualizing the Source of All Life: God as King, God as Guardian, God as Mother of the Cosmos. These are all attempts to wrap the transcendent Unknowable in words. This is one aspect of the experience we call God.[10]

THE CONTEXT

What exactly is a meditation? The term comes from the Latin *medi,* which means "center." As Rabbi David Zeller, the executive director of Yakar Institute of Jerusalem, writes, "It's a way to touch your center."[11] Rabbi Aryeh Kaplan defines it as "thinking in a controlled manner."[12] Rabbi Alan Lew speaks of it as "disciplined spirituality."[13] For Nan Fink Gefen, it is "a specific kind of activity that involves directing the mind."[14]

There are several Hebrew terms that correspond to meditation. The most general term is *kavanah,* which means "concentration" or "devotion." Rabbi Aryeh Kaplan renders it as "directed consciousness."[15] From the thirteenth century on, the Hebrew term *hitbonenut* (literally, "knowing oneself") appears in Kabbalistic literature. This refers to "protracted concentration of thought on supernal lights, of the divine world and of the spiritual worlds in general."[16] For Rabbi Kaplan, *hitbonenut,* self-understanding, is understanding oneself in the light of this vast creation.[17] According to Rabbi James L. Mirel and Karen B. Werth, it diminishes "the ego's power over the soul, which longs for union with God."[18]

Another term used for meditation is *devekut,* "clinging to," implying a need for the practitioner to reach a union with God (Deuteronomy 4:4). Some have used the expression *hitbodedut* as meaning "being alone" (understood as being alone with God). This self-isolation consists "in isolating the mind from all outward sensation and then even from thought itself."[19] Finally, there is the term *teshuvah,* which is usually translated as "return." But in mystical literature, it also means "a return to our essential nature."[20]

Gershom Scholem makes a distinction between Kabbalistic and Christian meditation. In Christian mysticism, he argues, "a pictorial and concrete subject, such as the suffering of Christ and all that pertains to it, is given to the meditator," whereas in the Kabbalah, "the subject is abstract and cannot be visualized, such as the Tetragrammaton and its combinations."[21] However, in many Jewish meditation practices today, it is not uncommon to focus on the letters of God's Holy Names.[22]

THE DIFFERENCE BETWEEN MEDITATION AND PRAYER

Meditation and prayer are not one and the same. One can meditate without praying, or pray without meditating. However, as Scholem notes, the hour of prayer is more suitable for meditation. He quotes the kabbalist Azriel of Gerona, in early thirteenth-century Spain, who wrote,

> The thought expands and ascends to its origin, so that when it reaches it, it ends and cannot ascend further...therefore the pious men of old raised their thoughts to its origin while pronouncing the precepts and words of prayer. As a result of this procedure and the state of adhesion which their thoughts attained, their words became blessed, multiplied, full of [divine] influx from the stage called the "nothingness of thought" just as the waters of a pool flow on every side when a man sets them free.[23]

It is unlikely that the rabbinic sages who composed the classical prayers in our liturgy consciously separated prayer from meditation and contemplation. For some, this is a question of emphasis. Rabbi Nachman of Breslov (1772–1811), the famous Hasidic teacher from Podolia and the Ukraine, made this distinction. When a person speaks to God spontaneously, it is a prayer, but when one makes it a fixed practice and spends definite times conversing with God, it is a meditation.[24] Some Jewish thinkers of our time make a similar distinction. For example, for Rabbi William Blank, a hypnotherapist and an author on spirituality, prayer is "talking to God," whereas meditation is "listening,"[25] that is, "a process of entering into an alternative state of consciousness."[26] Nan Fink Gefen says, "Prayer is our way of communicating with God. We raise our voices, or chant softly, or pray silently to convey what is in our hearts. Meditation is the way we enter the silence within. Although God is not directly addressed in this practice we experience profound moments of union with the Holy and the dissolution of the individual self, just as we do in prayer."[27]

For others, the distinction between prayer and meditation is not so clear, though most agree that they are frequently intertwined. Rabbi Steven A. Moss of B'nai Israel Reform Temple in Oakdale, New York, uses meditation as a preparation for the act of prayer. He writes, "I have found meditation to be one of the most valuable techniques for inspiring my prayer experience."[28] Some people meditate before prayer. Others integrate meditation into prayers. Some even pray after meditation as a way to continue to benefit from the meditation experience.

THE PURPOSE OF MEDITATION

Nan Fink Gefen writes that the reason why she adopted the discipline of meditation is that "I yearned to cultivate a spiritual practice that would infuse my daily existence with meaning."[29] It is universally accepted that meditation affords an individual the ability to deepen his or her spiritual growth. But it does more than that. One of the basic goals of meditation is to relax the mind and be in the present, leading to a higher level of consciousness. It can help us expand our consciousness by strengthening our powers of concentration. We become more balanced in our judgment. As Mindy Ribner, a meditation leader, warns us, "It is more than a stress reducer. It is the vehicle all religions use to impart the esoteric knowledge of their own mystical tradition."[30] Ultimately, meditation techniques "are meant to bring us to a direct experience of ourselves and of God."[31] Rabbi Steve Fisdel of B'nai Torach in Antioch, California, goes even further, "The true, primary objective of meditative practice within Jewish tradition is *yichud*, unification with God."[32] This mystical union is the ultimate goal for many people. Writes Avram Davis,

In every tradition, meditation is a way of focusing the consciousness in order to break through to a new level of understanding or being. In Judaism, the task of meditation is specifically to open the heart, to unclog the channel between the Infinite and the mortal. For the meditator "the soul becomes a throne for the Supernal Light above the head...and the light spreads around him and he is within the light, sitting and trembling with joy" (Keter Shem Tov, Aaron of Apt). This union with the Infinite is the most important thing.[33]

TYPES OF MEDITATION

Various types of meditation are used to expand one's consciousness. Allowing for a great deal of overlapping, we find different categories. Rabbi William Blank mentions five:[34]

1. Mantra: the repetition of a word or the name of God over and over again. This enables the practitioner to focus consciousness and connects the person with the sacred.

2. Mandala: a picture of various geometric figures. The idea is to direct oneself to the center of the figure as a means of concentration.

3. Movement: this includes dance and other physical activities.

4. Visualization: one brings to consciousness a particular image, usually a holy image.

5. Nothingness: ones clears the mind of everything, allowing the mind to receive influences that come from within or from without.

Rabbi Alan Lew counts three basic types of meditation:

1. Relaxation meditation, for the simple purpose of relaxation.

2. Trance meditation, during which one "leaves" one's ordinary state of mind.

3. Transformative meditation, which has a spiritual dimension.[35]

Avram Davis finds three "schools" of Jewish meditation that appear to be solidifying:

1. *Ayin* meditation: The Hebrew term *ayin* means "nothing" and refers to the notion that God is "no-thing." Therefore, in the words of Daniel Matt, professor of Jewish Spirituality at the Graduate Theological Union in Berkeley, California, it "animates all things and cannot be contained by any of them."[36] Avram Davis puts it this way: "This is the state of complete Oneness, by which is meant either God or the egoless state of a person who is in complete unity with God."[37]

2. *Hesed* (Hebrew for "benevolence," "love") meditation: the experience of *ayin* through lovingkindness.

3. Kabbalistic meditation: this relies on study, visualizations of God's names, and the recitation of some letters and names of power.

Nan Fink Gefen outlines three categories:[38]

1. Focused meditations, where the meditator concentrates on a single point, such as the breath, a word or phrase, a Jewish symbol, an image, or a sound.

2. Awareness meditation, wherein the mind is allowed to wander freely without a focus. Here the aim is to become more aware of the mental processes.

3. Emptiness meditation, which seeks to empty the mind of all thought. The meditator enters into a deep silence and experiences the *ayin*.

What happens during any of these meditations? Sylvia Boorstein, a senior teacher at the Insight Meditation Society in Barre, Massachusetts, shares the following experience:

> In periods of intensive meditation practice, at times when I have been very, very still, I've seen the world I know and recognize as myself and my story dissolve and become the vibrancy of infinite space.... As attention becomes focused, the habitual reflexive movements of the attention in response to stimuli become steadier, calmer; the tendency to cognize—to name things—diminishes. Things are just things. Life becomes deconstructed.... The place from which—or perhaps it's better to say, the process by means of which—the sentient, discriminating awareness of life begins, is revealed. It feels to me like the edge of creation.... If I spend some days in silence...the neuronal synapse-leaps that string stories together stop happening. My experience is *just* sounds. *Just* sensations. *Just* smells.... Not *boring*—plain. Actually, amazingly plain.[39]

MEDITATION TECHNIQUES

Just as there are different meditation types, there are also different ways of engaging in meditation. Some of them, as we saw, involve visualization; others include chanting, the repetition of words or sentences, even walking.

Meditation is a private exercise, as the Hebrew word *hitbodedut* ("being alone") implies. Therefore, each practitioner must find the best way that fits his or her personality and needs. Most people suggest that meditation should take place in the dark, or in a room that has little light, or in a place that offers serenity, relaxation, and peace of mind. It is also better to be comfortably seated.

Meditation could begin, for example, by focusing the mind

on one particular object or a word. To obtain the needed result—a heightened awareness of the spiritual realm, ultimately God—one must engage in "a discipline of surrender."[40] Preconceived ideas should be eliminated, foreign thoughts set aside, external distractions ignored, and the mind concentrated on a specific object or word. The length of meditation varies according to the meditator. Five minutes is a good start. Twenty minutes or half an hour is common.

Meditation, to be useful and productive, must be done on a regular basis. It cannot achieve its goal if it is done casually and without regularity. Besides, the practitioner must be comfortable with the technique chosen, and that requires practice and more practice. Ultimately, meditation must turn into a way of life. And one's entire life must turn into a meditation.

Of the numerous meditative techniques available to the practitioners, the following examples show how different they can be from one another. Most people start with a simple form of meditation and then move to a more demanding one. Beginners are urged to stay with one method for a while before moving to another. Some people use various techniques, depending on their particular need.

As part of one's self-examination, Rabbi James L. Mirel and Karen Bonnell Werth suggest a technique called *hitbonenut* ("self-understanding"):

> *Hitbonenut* meditation is a form of meditation used to understand the self in relationship to God's Creation…. Choose a single object of focus: a piece of bread, a leaf, an idea. Allow this object to fill your mind while moving beyond the object to its Source. You are like this object; the object becomes the mirror for you to see the Holy One that is beyond your self.[41]

Realizing that most people find it difficult to be fully present, Nan Fink Gefen recommends the *hineini* ("here I am") meditation:

Begin by taking a deep breath. As you exhale, make a sound…. Do this several times, then settle into your ordinary breathing.

Now watch your breath: Notice how your chest expands and contracts, and how your body receives the breath and lets it go. As you do this, your mind will begin to quiet down and you will start to relax.

When you are ready, move your attention to the word *hineini,* or, if you wish, to the words "Here I am."

Hineini. Here I am.

Focus on *hineini.*

Repeat it silently to yourself.

Hineini. Here I am.

Let the word become filled with your breath. Merge with it, so that you experience being fully present.

Hineini. Here I am.

Not thinking

Not accomplishing

Not doing

Just being.

Hineini. Here I am.

Full presence

Readiness to receive

In body

Heart

Mind

Spirit

Hineini. Here I am.

When your mind wanders, as it inevitably will, do not judge yourself. Simply notice where it has gone and return to *hineini.* If you are distracted by the sounds around you, notice them and return to *hineini.*

Hineini. Here I am.[42]

The following meditation by Tamar Frankiel and Judy Greenfeld is meant to help one reconnect one's soul with God as the source of light. It is to be said after the morning blessings:

Close your eyes. Breathe deeply. Visualize two *Shabbat* candles being lit. The match of inspiration touches the wick, and a flame ignites. The light spreads all around you, lighting the whole room. The radiant flame reaches upward toward its Creator and the world from which it came. The flame knows that it is here to light the world, and that when it is done, it will return to its Creator knowing it has fulfilled its purpose. Imagine yourself as this pure light, reaching toward God and shining out with knowledge and action to fulfill our work on earth. As you go through your day, remember your light, and see around you the lights of the others you encounter, all part of the One.[43]

Those who are more advanced might wish to try the next meditation, which was advocated by the thirteenth-century mystical teacher Abraham Abulafia. The use of the Hebrew letters provides an opportunity for the practitioner to receive God's abundant flow:

Prepare to meet your God.... Be totally alone.... Then take hold of ink, pen, and tablet.... Begin to combine [Hebrew]

letters, a few or many, permuting and revolving them rapidly
until your mind warms up. Delight in how they move and in
what you generate by revolving them. When you feel within
that your mind is very, very warm from combining the letters,
and that through the combinations you understand new things
that you have not attained by human tradition nor discovered
on your own through mental reflection, then you are ready to
receive the abundant flow, and the abundance flows upon
you, arousing you again and again.[44]

For Rabbi William Blank, meditation on a mandala, an image
of concentric geometric figures, can remind us that the individual and the universe are analogous. He prescribes the following
technique:

If you do not already have one, acquire a six-pointed star, a
Shield of David (Hebrew, *magen david*) charm.

Reflect on how this charm came into your possession, and
what special associations it holds for you.

Sit alone in a comfortable chair. Relax.

Stare at your charm for ten minutes. Focus your gaze so that
the charm is the only thing you see.

After meditation, reflect on the charm and its significance to
you.[45]

Rabbi Rami M. Shapiro, of the Sh'ma Centre at Temple Beth
Or, Miami, Florida, a center for meditation and spirituality,
speaks of his own meditative technique, based on Hasidic prece-
dents, as *avodah be-bittul,* the discipline of self-annihilation that
leads to the temporary ending of one's sense of self and sepa-
rateness. "All definitions and labels are erased," he notes, "and for
a moment you discover yourself to be what you truly are: God's
vehicle for knowing God as the Source and Substance of all re-

ality."[46] The practice of this type of meditation is rather simple: "No visualizations, no affirmations, no fantasies to occupy the mind and thrill the heart. Just sitting, breathing, and silently repeating a holy phrase."[47]

MEDITATION AS A PATH TO SPIRITUALITY

What is the expected result of this repeated exercise? Different meditators formulate their own views on this subject. Most of them, however, seem to share one general conclusion: meditation deepens our understanding, broadens our perspectives, and connects us to the Divine. For example, Rabbi David A. Cooper remarks, "The deeper we go into the experience of slowing down our busy minds, the more sensitive and aware we become of our surroundings. We begin to see hidden gems in everything we observe, and we discover new levels of appreciation in our daily lives. When we achieve more refined levels of awareness through quieting the mind, the result is an ever-deepening spiritual consciousness that opens the heart and renews the soul."[48]

Similarly, Rabbi Aryeh Kaplan writes, "The conversation with God becomes an awesome experience. As the conversation becomes easier and more relaxed, the experience deepens. It becomes a powerful meditative technique, which can easily bring one to higher states of consciousness. In these states of consciousness, God's presence becomes almost palpable."[49]

Maintaining that meditation is "the ending of thought," Rabbi Rami M. Shapiro tells us that "When thought returns and I am once more aware of myself as a separate self, I recognize profound changes. I am less tense and more composed. My thought processes are less rigid and a little more subtle. The world I sense around me seems more alive: colors are more vibrant, sounds are more sweet, the details of things seem to stand out more vividly. There is a joy that accompanies me when I return from meditative practice."[50]

Rabbi Steve Fisdel says that when we reconnect with God through meditation, "we unite ourselves with the Source of all being and come to understand the greater dimensions of our lives."[51] Meditation can be, and often is, tranformative. Writes Avram Davis, "It can bring us to a greater joy and inner freedom."[52] Rabbi William Blank finds that as a result of meditation "You are more relaxed and happier, or able to better express your emotions, or perceive sensory images."[53] Similarly, Tamar Frankiel and Judy Greenfeld, in their book on the practice of meditation, maintain that "The more you commit to these prayers, exercises, and meditations over time, the greater the changes you will see in yourself. Your hunger for external satisfaction will diminish. You will want to exercise more, eat healthy foods, and open your mind to spiritual learning. The only 'hunger' that increases is your yearning for deeper spirituality.... You will be able to feel your natural heartbeat, or the presence of God.... You will, in short, become transparent to your soul."[54]

Nan Fink Gefen, who considers meditation "a vehicle for profound personal and spiritual change," maintains that the change comes through progressive stages: concentration leads to awareness, this brings us greater knowledge of self, and ultimately we realize that we are part of the unfolding of life.[55] Rabbi Steven A. Moss tells us that he follows a daily discipline of meditation and finds that "not only [does it] enhance the spirituality of my prayer, but opens channels to the Divine which become useful for the entire day."[56]

However, it must be said clearly that the contemplative life is not for everyone. Not all have the predisposition for this kind of activity. Rabbi Jonathan Omer-Man, the founder of Metivta, a Jewish school of wisdom and meditation, warns that one must avoid becoming addicted to "highs" and that at times meditation may have its "dry period" when it leads nowhere. This may even cause a loss of meaning in life, and therefore the practitioner must rediscover meaning.[57] Furthermore, because meditation requires discipline, it becomes at times difficult if not painful. Rabbi David A. Cooper gives us an example:

> This morning's meditation was agony. I have been trying a new style of pure silence—sitting quietly without any mantra, observing the breath, or working with visualization or focal point exercises. In earliest retreats I could chant for hours without any problem; in fact the chanting usually led to ecstasy. I could also do breathing exercises all day and attain a sublime state. But sitting perfectly still, focusing on emptiness, doing nothing, thinking nothing, is pure hell. Pain racks my upper back, radiating from the spine to the shoulders.[58]

For many people, meditation is very useful not only for individual spiritual growth for self-improvement, but also for the betterment of society. Kennard Lipman, a teacher of meditation, reminds us that "Meditation practices implement a view or a way of seeing. This means that meditation literally builds worlds and determines behavior."[59] Ultimately, meditative activities enable the individual to change and become a better human being, able to take more from the world and willing to give more to the world. Meditation, when done properly and according to a rigorous routine, writes Rabbi David Zeller, "aims to fix and elevate this world, to sacralize the everyday."[60]

CHAPTER 7

Spirituality through Ritual

To celebrate the sacred, we create rituals.
—Rabbi Morris N. Kertzer

T HE SACRED REALM, which pervades a good portion of our
lives, contains certain holy acts that are powerful tools for
spiritual expression. Thousands of people consider these sanctified deeds as a primary path of their personal spirituality. Why
are people attracted to these religious rituals? What place does
ritual play within Judaism? We now turn to a more detailed study
of these matters.

RITUAL AND RELIGION

Human beings are creatures of habit. We tend to do certain things
over and over in the same manner. For example, we follow the
same routine when we dress ourselves. We comb our hair in the
same fashion. We tend to write, drive, or eat exactly the same way
day after day. These repeated actions are our second nature. They
define us.

There are other acts that we all carry out because they have
become shared rituals in our social life. We salute the flag. We
shake hands. We put a hand over the heart when we say the
Pledge of Allegiance. We stand up when we sing the national an-

them. We applaud a performing artist. We light birthday candles. We hug and kiss on one side of the face. These are secular acts mandated by local custom.

In addition to these habitual acts, most religions have their own rituals, which are prescribed by sacred law, custom, or religious leaders. Though it is not always easy to differentiate these rituals from their secular counterparts, a few observations may help us accomplish this task. Secular ceremonies are like a show, carried out for the sake of onlookers. In fact, they are "performed" for the pleasure of the audience. They take place within a secular social context. Religious rituals, on the other hand, have an internal quality. They heighten the soul. They are carried out, mostly during religious times and places, in response to a presumed higher authority: sacred tradition and/or God. Thus, for example, a *bar mitzvah* candidate on the pulpit is not performing for the audience, but is leading the service as a *shaliah tzibbur* (a "representative of the congregation") in fulfillment of a religious discipline. The person who blows the *shofar* (ram's horn) during a Jewish holy day is not simply playing a musical instrument but is complying with a biblical command.[1]

Though religious rituals may vary from place to place, they usually mark life-cycle events, seasonal changes, holy days, or community celebrations. "Without ritual…" writes Rabbi Wayne Dosick, "there is an emptiness, a hollowness, to our lives. We are without anchor at points where life insists on rootedness and source, without touchstone when we long for the familiar; we are without identity in a world where our sense of unique meaning and purpose is easily lost."[2]

However, some people argue that rituals stifle religious expression. They are not required in theological discourse. "Why do I need to light candles," these people say, "if I already understand and appreciate what these candles stand for? Is the actual deed necessary?" In answer to this, Rabbi Morris Kertzer (1910–1983) writes,

To say such ceremonies are superfluous is to say that words
can get along without music, or that having prose, we need
no poetry. But words alone become "wordy," and prose is
"prosaic." Music and poetry, on the other hand, raise the casual to the important and the humdrum to the exalted. Rituals
lend symbolic poetry to life; they are the music of our souls;
they provide the inner passion without which life becomes
hardly worth continuing.[3]

Many who consider themselves religious are also observant of
religious rituals. However, some people practice certain religious
rituals without identifying themselves as religious. They may practice the rituals simply out of habit or just to be part of a community rather than out of a theological conviction. And some, like
the Jewish philosopher Martin Buber, are highly religious without being observant. In reality, ritual and religion are not one and
the same. Religion encompasses much more than ritual or observance. Most religions include a ritual discipline but are not defined
exclusively by it. Religion also deals with matters of belief, which
are not always manifested through particular acts.

MITZVOT IN JUDAISM

Over the centuries, Jewish sages have created many rituals that
are part of the practice of Judaism. For example, we light Sabbath
candles. We blow the *shofar*. We kiss the Torah scrolls. We eat
matzah during Passover. We shake the *lulav* on Sukkot. These religious ceremonial acts, codified in biblical and rabbinic texts, are
part of a wider system of *mitzvot* (pl. of *mitzvah*) that had been
developed since early biblical times. Therefore, in order to understand the role of ritual in Judaism, we must first study the general concept of *mitzvah* in Jewish sources.

Though most people translate the word *mitzvah* as "good
deed," there is a major difference between a good deed and a

mitzvah. A good deed is voluntary. The basic root of the word *mitzvah,* however, is "commandment." It implies an obligatory act. The "Statement of Principles for Reform Judaism" (1999) renders it as "sacred obligation."

There is a new tendency to extend the meaning of this word and to see in *mitzvah* an element of connection. Basing his argument on the mystical assumption that everything in the universe is related to everything else, Rabbi Arthur Waskow, one of the leading thinkers of the Jewish Renewal movement, writes, "We understand the *mitzvot* not as commandments but as connections."4 He adds, "Seeing *mitzvot* as connections opens up to a sense of the world in which God is not a Commander but the Web of Connections that makes a Unity of the universe."5 Similarly, Tamar Frankiel and Judy Greenfeld remark, "The word *mitzvah* tells us: Make a connection. We don't have to think of *mitzvot* as a grand system in which you have to do everything, or do nothing. In any given moment, we can act in a way that *connects.* Sometimes we connect to God, sometimes to ourselves, sometimes to other people. In any moment, you can turn your face toward God's light, and experience *teshuvah,* a 'return.' In any moment, you can shine your own light toward someone else and help transform your life and theirs."6

The theological question that needs to be raised here has to do with the identity of the *meztaveh,* the commanding voice, behind the *mitzvah.* Who is it? For some, the commander is God, however defined. For others, it is Jewish history; that is to say, *mitzvot* emerge out of the experience of the Jewish people. There are also those who maintain that reality itself—or better, the physical and spiritual laws governing reality—are at the root of each *mitzvah.*7

The rabbis of the past identified 613 *mitzvot* altogether for which Jews are responsible. These days, it is not possible to observe all of these *mitzvot,* for the simple reason that some of these obligatory acts can be carried out only in the Land of Israel and some only by the priests in the ancient Temple of Jerusalem. Therefore, in practical terms, there are only about 200 *mitzvot* that an observant Jew in the Diaspora can now practice in daily life.

THE PURPOSE OF THE *MITZVOT*

At times, the rationale for the performance of a *mitzvah* contains a built-in reward. For example, in the Decalogue, we read: "Honor your father and your mother, that you may long endure on the land which the Lord your God is giving you" (Exodus 20:12; Deuteronomy 5:16 adds "and that you may fare well"). Similarly, the law enjoins the farmer to leave the forgotten sheaves for the poor by promising God's blessings (Deuteronomy 24:19). In other cases, obedience is obtained "so that no plague may come upon" the Israelites (see Exodus 30:12; Leviticus 19:17; Deuteronomy 20:18). Some laws contain "motive clauses" that attempt to promote compliance by providing an explanation that appeals to the mind or heart. For example, taking bribes is prohibited because "bribes blind the clear-sighted and upset the plans of the just" (Exodus 23:8; Deuteronomy 16:19). Many laws contain motivating clauses of a historical nature: "You shall not wrong a stranger or oppress him, for you were strangers in the land of Egypt." And many laws are simply based on God's commanding authority, for example, "You shall not make gashes in your flesh for the dead, or incise any marks on yourselves: I am the Lord" (Leviticus 19:28).[8]

In the rabbinic literature, the purpose of the *mitzvot* continued to occupy the minds of the sages. Thus, an ancient midrash stresses the following:

> The *mitzvot* were given to Israel only in order that people should be purified *[letzaref]* through them. For, what does it matter to God whether a beast is slain at the throat or at the neck [as the Jewish law requires]. (Gen. R. 44:1)

Similarly, in an answer to Tarnus Rufus, the governor of Judea, Rabbi Akiba told him that the reason circumcision of males is required is that God gave Israel *mitzvot* in order "to refine *[letzaref]*" them (Tanh., Tazria, 5).

Specific rewards and punishments accompany many rabbinic laws or injunctions. For example, according to the sages, "the charitable will have children that are healthy and wise" (BB 9b). Furthermore, in many laws, the rabbis tell us, the reward will come to us not in this world but in the world to come. Thus, according to the Mishnah,

> These are the things whose fruits a person enjoys in this world and while the capital is laid up for him in the world to come: honoring father and mother, deeds of lovingkindness, making peace between one another, and the study of Torah is equal to all of them. (Peah 1:1)

Yet, in spite of this teaching, many of the ancient rabbis taught that this is not the ideal. One should really perform a *mitzvah* because of its intrinsic value, not because of the merit attached to it. For, as Antigonos of Sokho said, "Be not like servants who work for their master on condition that they would receive payment, but, on the contrary, be like servants who labor for their master without expecting a reward" (Av. 1:3). Similarly, Ben Azzai insisted that "the reward of a *mitzvah* is another, just as the failure to observe a commandment leads to another" (Av. 4:2).

Similar sentiments are expressed today. Michael Strassfeld, the editor of the best-selling *Jewish Catalog,* writes elsewhere, "As later Judaism came to lay stress on the *mitzvot* in all their detail, it became easy to think of Torah as a point system for collecting merit badges from the Great Scoutmaster in the sky. In such a system, it is easy to forget that the real purpose of the *mitzvot* is to help us 'to become a kingdom of priests and a holy nation' and to maintain a covenant with the living God."9 For Avram Davis, the role of the *mitzvot* is even higher: "All of the *mitzvot* (spiritual practices) are ultimately designed to further this rapturous attachment *(devekut)* [to God]."[10]

No matter what the rationale for the *mitzvot*, ultimately they are not to be viewed as a burden or a hardship. Commenting on the biblical verse "Being bound up in their clothes upon their shoulders" (Exodus 12:34), Rabbi Nathan asks, how come the Israelites had to carry their kneading bowls? Didn't they have beasts of burden with them? The answer is: "The Israelites simply cherished [*mehavevin*] their religious duties [*mitzvotam*]" (Mek., Pisha, 13). *Mitzvot* enable the individual to experience the goodness of life and to express gratitude to God. For observant Jews, the performance of *mitzvot* represents a heightening of one's consciousness. "If you understand *mitzvot*," writes Michael Lerner, "as the attempt by a community to fulfilll what is learned to be its revolutionary obligations and to keep alive the message of liberation and transformation, you can understand why the Jew saw *mitzvah* as conferring dignity."[11] In the eyes of the rabbinic sages, *mitzvot* reflect the love of God for the people of Israel. In the liturgy, they are "are our life and the length of our days." And according to Rabbi Hananniah ben Akashya, "The Holy One, blessed be He, wanted to give merit to Israel, therefore He increased for them Torah and *mitzvot*, as it is written, 'The Lord desires His [servant's] vindication, that he may magnify and glorify [His] teaching' (Isaiah 42:21)" (Mek. 3:16; Av. 6:11).

TYPES OF *MITZVOT*

It is customary to divide the *mitzvot* into two major categories. Some deal with positive acts *(mitzvot 'aseh)* and others with negative deeds *(mitzvot lo ta'aseh)*. For example, "Honor your father and mother" (Exodus 20:12) and "You shall rise before the aged and show deference to the old" (Deuteronomy 19:32) are part of the positive *mitzvot*. On the other hand, "You shall not defraud your neighbor" (Leviticus 19:13) and "You shall not steal" (Exodus 20:13) represent two of the negative *mitzvot*.

Not all the *mitzvot* deal with ritual matters. Some, in fact, cover interpersonal relations. Consequently, many people distinguish between ethical and ritual *mitzvot*. The first are referred to as *mitzvot ben adam lahavero* ("*mitzvot* between a person and his or her fellow"), whereas ritual *mitzvot* are called *ben adam lamakom* ("between a person and the [holy] abode"). "Do not take bribes" (Exodus 23:8) is a *mitzvah ben adam lahavero*, whereas "Three times a year you shall hold a festival for Me" (Exodus 23:14) is a *mitzvah ben adam lamakom.*

In his book, *A Jewish Theology*, Rabbi Louis Jacobs of England, a Conservative rabbi, provides the following way of categorizing the *mitzvot*:[13]

1. The Significant. Here, the author includes such *mitzvot* as the dietary laws, the Sabbath, *tallit*, *tefillin* and *mezuzah*, Yom Kippur and the other festivals, stressing that "the religious ideals of holiness and life's spiritual enrichment are enhanced by the observances."

2. The Meaningless. Here, Rabbi Jacobs cites *mitzvot* such as the laws of shaving and *sha'atnez* (the mixing of two kinds of seeds or clothing; see Deuteronomy 22:11; Leviticus 19:19), which were perhaps reflective of the protest against idolatrous practices in the past.

3. The Harmful. Here, he mentions the laws that discriminate against women.

Early Reform Jews gave priority to ethical over ceremonial laws. In fact, the Pittsburgh Platform, adopted in 1885, clearly stated that

> We recognize in the Mosaic legislation a system of training the Jewish people for its mission during the national life in Palestine, and today we accept as binding only the moral laws and maintain only such ceremonies as elevate and sanctify our lives, but reject all such as are not adapted to the views and habits of modern civilization.

Yet, this distinction is not always clear, for there is a great deal of crossover between the two. As Rabbi Joseph Telushkin, a prolific writer associated with CLAL, the National Jewish Center for Learning and Leadership, points out, "With regard to the laws of the Sabbath, a set of regulations that the people normally regard as purely ritual, the Torah commands that one's servants be freed from work on that day. Is that a ritual or an ethical ordinance? Clearly, the distinction between ritual and ethical laws is far from absolute."[12]

By the middle of the 1930s, Reform Jews had made enormous strides in their appreciation of the importance of religious ceremonies as powerful means of expressing religious fervor. The Columbus Platform of 1937 includes the following statement:

> Judaism as a way of life requires in addition to its moral and spiritual demands, the preservation of the Sabbath, festivals, and Holy Days, the retention and development of such customs, symbols, and ceremonies as possess inspirational value, the cultivation of distinctive forms of religious art and music, and the use of Hebrew, together with the vernacular, in our worship and instruction.

The horizon was broadened even further in the 1970s. The "Centenary Perspective" of the Central Conference of American Rabbis (1976) stresses that

> Within each area of Jewish observance Reform Jews are called upon to confront the claims of Jewish tradition, however differently perceived, and to exercise their individual autonomy, choosing and creating on the basis of commitment and knowledge.

In the "Statement of Principles for Reform Judaism," Reform Jews are now "committed to the study of the *whole array of mitzvot* (emphasis added) and to the fulfillment of those that address us as individuals and as a community."

The difference between *mitzvot* carried out by Orthodox Jews and those observed by non-Orthodox Jews is found not so much in the number of *mitzvot* but in the theological foundations that underlie them. Generally speaking, one can say that

1. Orthodox Jews observe *mitzvot* because they are God's will. Non-Orthodox Jews practice them because *mitzvot*, human creations as they are, represent our attempt to reach the Divinity.

2. Orthodox Jews stress uniformity in religious observance; non-Orthodox Jews prefer diversification.

3. Orthodox Jews are expected to be scrupulous in their practice; non-Orthodox Jews consider *mitzvot* as means to a higher end and therefore accept individual expression.

4. Orthodox Jews don't look favorably upon change in the performance of *mitzvot;* non-Orthodox Jews would sanction change as a way to respond to present needs.

In spite of all these differences, no matter what theological rationale stands behind the practice of *mitzvot*, the large majority of Jews are united in their assumption that it is the practice of *mitzvot* that strengthens our sense of belonging and loyalty to the Jewish people. In other words, we are Jews not only because we believe in One God—others do, too!—but primarily because we share the same history and the same tradition, and particularly because we perform mostly the same religious rituals.

WIDENING THE CONCEPT OF *MITZVOT*

In response to present needs, Jewish thinkers of our time, inspired by the spirit of Torah, are insisting on widening the scope of the *mitzvot*. Let me mention just two examples.

New and Reclaimed Women's Rituals

Under the influence of many Jewish feminist thinkers, women are now taking upon themselves the obligation to carry out many more *mitzvot* and perform more rituals. Among the non-Orthodox, they are studying for the rabbinate and the cantorate in larger numbers than ever before. They are teaching Torah to students in all levels of schooling. Many congregations sponsor Rosh Chodesh groups that meet once a month for prayer, study, and fellowship.

Older rituals are constantly being reevaluated in light of this new development, in order to give voice to present needs. For example, *On the Doorpost of Your House,* a home prayer book published by the Central Conference of American Rabbis in 1994, contains prayers and ceremonies for such situations as fear of infertility, learning of a pregnancy, menstruation, and bringing a new child home.[14]

However, this trend has its critics. Francine Klagsbrun writes, "I have reservations about new rituals some women have developed that focus on body functions, such as ceremonies for menarche in a young woman or menopause in an older one. They seem to return to the days when society defined women by their biological makeup and restricted them because of it."[15]

Eco-*Kashrut*

There is a greater tendency these days to view the laws of *kashrut* much more broadly than before. The Hebrew word *kasher* means "fit" for consumption. The Bible and the rabbinic codes have compiled many laws that deal with what an observant Jew can or cannot eat.[16] The Biblical rationale for these laws is "holiness." In essence, *kashrut* is seen as a personal discipline that leads to a spiritual awareness of God's presence even during an ordinary act of eating. Contemporary Jewish thinkers offer the rationales of ethics, Jewish nationalism, and personal spiritual development to support its observance.

Along with the increased interest in vegetarianism, there is greater interest in dealing with what many people call eco-*kashrut*. As Rabbi Arthur Green remarks, "Food and other domestic products produced either by severely oppressed workers or at the cost of serious damage to the environment are also being questioned as extensions of the principles of *kashrut*."[17]

PROPER INTENTION

As with prayers, the observance of a *mitzvah* requires *kavanah*: concentration and the appropriate intent to do it right. As Rabbi Tirzah Firestone noted, "Judaism is designed to come alive through *mitzvot*, or practices, but those practices must be done with an open, listening heart if they are to lead one into an elevated consciousness. Actions that are done automatically, outside an active relationship with the living God, can grow dead and useless."[18]

Thus, according to Jewish law, for example,

If a person was passing behind a house of worship...and heard the sound of the Shofar...if he has directed his heart he has fulfilled his obligation, but if he did not, he has not fulfilled his duty. (R.H. 3:7)

According to Jewish tradition, when you are ready to do a *mitzvah*, first you recite a prayer, as if to say, "I am aware of the importance of this deed and am prepared to do it for its own sake" (namely, *lishmah*), and then you carry out the act.[19] In fact, in many Hasidic circles, there is even a statement to be recited before the recitation of such a prayer: "*Hineni mukhan umezuman lekayyem...*" (Here, I am ready to perform [the *mitzvah* of...]). Rabbi Louis Jacobs wrote, "*Kavanah* keeps the *mitzvot* from becoming mechanical; *lishmah* prevents us from showing off or patting ourselves on the back when we do what is right."[20]

RITUAL AS A PATH TO SPIRITUALITY

Within the array of the *mitzvot*, those designated as *ben adam lamakom* ([commandments] between a person and the [holy] abode) often become the means by which many people seek to express their spirituality. We can see the connection between *mitzvot* and ritual in the following example. On Friday evening, a Jewish family is getting ready to welcome Shabbat. They sit at their festive table. First they light the Sabbath candles, then they recite the blessing over the wine, and finally they say the *motzi,* the blessing over bread. They wish each other *"Shabbat Shalom"* and proceed to have a lovely meal. After dinner, they recite a prayer of gratitude for the food and then sing Sabbath songs.

This scene may be familiar to many Jews, but it is a new experience for others who are searching for a meaningful way to express their religious sentiments. Often, individuals who discover Judaism anew or wish to assume it as a personal and spiritual discipline adopt the observance of the *mitzvot* as a first step on the road to a full Jewish religious life. Most people need to translate their religious beliefs into concrete acts and find that ritual is an effective way to accomplish this goal. It gives them a sense of personal satisfaction of doing something for a higher cause. It becomes a method of self-transcendence, a means of reaching the Divine. Thus, Rabbi Lawrence A. Hoffman writes,

> Ritual is a human art form that can transform as well as maintain, liberate as well as oppress. We need, therefore, to return to ritual as a human penchant for pattern akin to God's initial act of creation; and to see how ritual can lead equally to a new and positive creative order in the process we call *tikkun olam.* The key to understanding ritual in all its potential is to see God as the first ritualizer, God the Creator telling us by the example of Genesis that we too must exercise our God-like creativity.[21]

THE FUNCTIONS OF JEWISH RITUAL

In Judaism, rituals basically play four functions: educational, emotional, communal, and theological or existential. Let us study each separately.

The Educational Role of Ritual

A few years back, at a Jewish summer camp, I asked the participants what they expected to take back home at the end of the session. Several of them lamented the fact that they could not share with their families some of the religious experiences we had in those few weeks. One young man wrote, "I'd like to have services twice a day with my family, but I feel I cannot accomplish this goal, because my family is not religious."

A young woman said, "One thing that I would like to bring back, but I can't, is a nice Shabbat meal together."

Another camper lamented, "I think I'd like to bring back the lighting of the candles. It makes me feel good. But I will not be able to get the family together for this."

Yet another one said, "I would like to do *Havdalah* at home, but my family doesn't know enough about it, and it just doesn't fit into our daily activities, although I wish it did."

As congregational rabbis we often hear from parents who tell us that in the religious school their children are learning about certain Jewish rituals that were not part of their own family life. Because the parents have never celebrated these rituals before, they feel strange about them. Besides, they say, they would not even know how to carry out the rituals at home. Here is where a good teacher comes in.

Rituals are not difficult to perform. Most of them deal with simple concrete acts. They can be done at home, in the synagogue, or in the marketplace. They are often repeated under similar conditions, and, as we know, repetition is important in learning a skill. Teachers can demonstrate them to their students: this is how you give *tzedakah;* this is how you light the Sabbath candles; this is how you blow the *shofar.* By so doing, they not only sharpen the skills of the participants but also make them feel comfortable with the ritual itself and teach important aspects of Judaism. With practice, rituals often become second nature and part of our daily routine.

In addition to teaching a skill, teachers can also use rituals to highlight Jewish values. For example, they can point out that the wine used during *kiddush* is more than simple wine. It stands for joy in Jewish life, as we read, "Wine cheers the heart of people" (Psalms 104:15). And what better time to proclaim joy than during the Sabbath, which the Bible knows as *oneg* (a "delight," Isaiah 58:13). In fact, in the rabbinic literature, the entire day is viewed as "a taste of paradise" (Ber. 57b). In the *Zohar* it is described as "a mirror of the world to come" (Gen. 48a). It is no wonder that we are enjoined to celebrate the Sabbath with special rituals.

The Emotional Role of Ritual

Rituals often evoke high emotions. The objects we use during a ritual can bring up a memory or remind us of important people in our lives. When we light the Sabbath candles, for example, we may remember our parents; the seder plate may recreate a scene from another time or place. This ritual act connects us not only to our tradition but also to our families and friends.

During a ritual, the symbols we use also carry a meaning beyond themselves. They stand for certain values, goals, and aspirations. As such, they elevate the moment and create a sacred memory. For instance, during the wedding ceremony, the wedding ring functions as more than an ordinary round band. It becomes a symbol of love uniting husband and wife. The breaking of the glass at the end of the wedding is infused with all kinds of meaning, from remembering the destruction of the Temple of

Jerusalem to the realization that life's fragility will be balanced by the love between the couple.[22] Rabbi Morris Kertzer wrote, "Rituals invest 'ordinary' acts and things with symbolic meaning, thus moving us beyond the ordinary to the holy. They relate ourselves and what we do to the Source of our being."[23]

The Communal Role of Ritual

When people share the same ritual, a community is formed. Thus, for example, when we recite the *motzi* and break bread together, a special bond is established among those who are present. This connection can also be extended to those who are beyond our immediate horizon. By attending a Passover seder, a Jew quickly realizes that other Jews are doing pretty much the same thing all over the world. They may read the *haggadah* in different languages or taste slightly different type of *haroset*, but they are all reciting the same story of the Exodus. Similarly, when we read or chant the Torah on Shabbat morning, we become aware of the fact that the same portion is being read or chanted in all the synagogues of the Diaspora. This awareness is enough to connect one Jew to another in kinship and a religious bond.

The Theological/Existential Role of Ritual

Rituals point to something higher. They connect us with a source of power beyond ourselves. They remind us of our place in the universe. They make us aware of the presence of God, helping us to articulate words of gratitude, acceptance, or praise. When used as a special spiritual path, they, like other *mitzvot*, "refine" us as individuals and as members of the Jewish community. The rituals that recall the great historic events of the past, such as the seder, or dwelling in the *sukkah*, reawaken within us strong sentiments of religious and moral idealism. Rabbi Milton Steinberg (1903–1950) wrote:

A key objective of Judaism...is the sanctification of life. Every moment, the Tradition contends, ought to be suffused with the awareness of God and with moral fervor. To this end each turn of man's existence should be accompanied by acts evocative of religious and ethical idealism. Under this conception, Jewish ritual is intended as a spiritualizing device, a kind of persistent and all-pervading whispering of the verse in Numbers (15:39): "and ye shall look upon this and remember all the commandments of the Lord."[24]

· The observance of ritual *mitzvot* does not always come easily or naturally. However, as one becomes accustomed to the ritual, the action takes on a deeper meaning and purpose, ultimately elevating the ordinary act to something special. To this end, the rabbis have long insisted that rituals should also be performed with beauty in mind. They called this *hiddur mitzvah* ("the adornment of the commandment"). When you use a ritual object, they taught, it should be as elegant as possible. The *etrog* used during Sukkot should be of a fine quality (S.H. Orah Hayyim, #656). The *ketubah* at the wedding should be a work of art, not a scrawny piece of paper. The *kiddush* cup should be made of precious material, not a Dixie cup. People should take pride in the ritual objects they use; often these objects are inherited from older generations and are in turn transmitted to children and grandchildren.

For some people carrying out a ritual in a prescribed manner and using such beautiful objects of art becomes the highest form of religiosity, the spiritual path that connects them to the Divine. In other words, the *mitzvah* is transformed into a spiritual medium of the highest order. Ron Wolfson, the director of the Whizin Institute for Jewish Family Life at the University of Judaism, writes the following:

It has always amazed me how much time is spent teaching "about" Judaism and not how to "do" Judaism. My audience has not, by and large, grown up with Jewish ritual practice in their homes. And, if they did, they hardly know why they do what they do when they "do Jewish." So, I spend a lot of time actually modeling the ritual behaviors I'm teaching. I light the candles, I break the *matzah,* and I spin the *dreidle.* When I teach the chant of a *berakhah,* I sing the loudest. I constantly provide a model for the learner to follow. A rabbi once told me it was "beneath" him to teach this way. He wanted to teach spirituality to his people. Well, guess what? It's no accident that the center of "spirituality" is "ritual." I suppose there are other ways to find God, but, for me, and most of the students I work with, ritual behavior is the fundamental path to spirituality.[25]

Rabbi Jacob Neusner, a prominent rabbinic scholar of our time, expresses a similar sentiment about ritual when he writes, "I practice Judaism because only in the practice of the faith do I gain access to what the faith conveys, which is knowledge of God as God wishes to be known."[26]

Many Jews agree with this position and feel that the act of doing a *mitzvah,* whether it is one between a person and God or between one person and another, connects them to the Divine. As Rabbi Marcia Prager writes, "With each *mitzvah* we affirm that we live consciously within the flow of God and intend each of our actions to be yet another window into the fullness of the Divine Presence."[27] In and of itself, this is a religious deed and a spiritual pathway.

CHAPTER 8

Spirituality through Relationship and Good Deeds

Wash yourselves clean;
Put your evil doings
Away from My sight.
Cease to do evil;
Learn to do good.
Devote yourselves to justice;
Aid the wronged.
Uphold the rights of the orphan;
Defend the cause of the widow.
—Isaiah 1:16–17

HUMAN BEINGS ARE SOCIAL ANIMALS. We live together. We need one another. We depend on one another. Especially in Judaism, community plays a great role. Hillel the Elder urges us not to separate ourselves from the community (Av. 2:4). Rabbinic law requires ten males (and among liberal Jews, women too) to make up a quorum for prayer. The community then becomes the context for personal spirituality. And this is where many people find their own personal spiritual path. How can relationship or good deeds lead a person to spiritual heights? What does Judaism teach about the performance of deeds of lovingkindness as a way to express religious commitment? Though this emphasis is not unique to Judaism, it does play a dominant role in the rabbinic teachings.

To understand the place that these *mitzvot ben adam lahavero* ("between a person and his or her fellow") have within Judaism, we must go back to the ancient world. In the ancient Near East, almost every natural phenomenon was considered a divinity in its own right. For example, Hadad (or Adad) was the storm god; Shamash (or Utu) was the sun god; Sin (or Nanna) was the moon god; Ishtar (or Inanna) was the goddess of fertility. Each city also had its own god or goddess: Enlil was the god of Nippur; Marduk was the god of Babylon; An was the god of Uruk.

In the Hebrew Bible, YHVH is the God of Israel and, following the pattern of the ancient Near Eastern divinities, the author of Psalm 29 saw in the power of nature the clear hand of Israel's God:

> The voice of the Lord is over the waters; the God of glory thunders, the Lord, over the mighty waters. (Psalms 29:3)

However, elsewhere in the Bible is the belief that the Israelite God acted through historical events as well. Though this idea is not an Israelite innovation, it is paramount for the understanding of the role of YHVH. For example, several places in the Bible, we read:

> I the Lord am your God who brought you out of the land of Egypt, the house of bondage. (Exodus 20:2, 13:3ff.; Amos 2:1–11; Isaiah 45:1ff)

The fact that the God of Israel acts through history enabled the Israelites to see YHVH as a personal God who had a relationship with them through a covenant, and therefore took a personal interest in their well-being. This is not a faraway God but a God who is a loving parent. Thus, in the Song of Moses, the poet tells us that God loves the Israelites as if they were God's own children:

He found him in a desert region,

In an empty howling waste.

He engirded him, watched over him,

Guarded him as the pupil of His eye.

(Deuteronomy 21:10)

This love affair between God and Israel began with the patriarchs and extends to all of their progeny: "And because He
loved your fathers [the three patriarchs Abraham, Isaac, and
Jacob], He chose their heirs after them" (Deuteronomy 4:37).
This caring and personal relationship has become a paradigm of
the relationship that must exist between one person and another.

In our time, many people seek and find spirituality not only
by being in awe of natural phenomena, or through rational discourse, but primarily through relationship with others and by
means of good deeds toward their fellow human beings. For
some, this is one of several possible avenues; for others, it is a
dominant portion of their spirituality. Judaism puts a high priority on this matter. As Michael Lerner indicates, "Judaism places
transcendence on the agenda of the human race. Human beings
need not be stuck in a world of pain or oppression. We can regain contact with a deeper level of being.... Much of the pain and
oppression we experience in this world is a reflection of the way
we do not recognize God in the world, in one another, in ourselves."[1] When we extend ourselves to others, we can draw from
the values we associate with the Divine and improve the world
around us. This is the highest kind of religious expression.

THE LIFE OF DIALOGUE

The German Jewish philosopher Martin Buber (1878–1965) built
his entire philosophical approach on the idea of relationship and
genuine dialogue. As we have already discussed, Buber main-

tained that we usually relate to one another as I-It, a relationship of "experiencing and using." But Buber also argued that once in a while, we are fortunate to enter into a higher level of relationship: I-Thou. Here there is "mutual confirmation." One party does not judge or use the other. In a genuine dialogue, writes Buber, "each of the participants really has in mind the other or others in their present and particular being, and turns to them with the intention of establishing a living mutual relation between himself and them."[2]

Every time we enter into an I-Thou relationship, says Buber, we also get a glimpse of the eternal Thou, who is God. In his words, "in every Thou we address the eternal Thou."[3] In that respect, every true relationship is also a dialogue with God. In Buber's words, "The relation to a human being is the proper metaphor for the relation to God."[4]

The I-Thou meeting is not everlasting. As soon as one is aware of this relationship, judgment intervenes and the contact turns into an I-It. However, the meeting is not without a positive result. According to Buber, we step out of this contact with a definite gain. We become more sensitive, more understanding, and more human. We can return to work with more insight, even though there is no clear mandate of how to translate this insight into specific acts. "Man receives," Buber writes, "and what he receives is not a 'content' but a presence, a presence as strength."[5] This presence, he adds, contains three elements: "the whole abundance of actual reciprocity," "the confirmation of meaning," and, finally, the confirmation that this meaning "is not of 'another life,' but that of this life."[6] Buber urges us to try to relate to others with genuineness and with mutuality. For this to happen we don't need to renounce the world. On the contrary, it is within the context of our everyday life that we can find that special spiritual relationship.

In discussing his personal spirituality, Rabbi Paul Menitoff, the executive vice-president of the Central Conference of American Rabbis, writes,

I struggle between a belief in God as a power, rather than a personality, who is manifest through natural law and a belief in a God who seems to have a personal interest in me and who intercedes in my life. I am at a loss to describe the attributes of this God, and have adopted a quasi-Buberian view that I can only experience this God through my relationships with others.... Both manifestations of God are very real to me.[7]

An echo of this kind of thinking is found in the poem "Between," composed by Rabbi Harold Schulweis, a creative thinker and rabbi of Valley Beth Shalom congregation in Encino, California, which includes these lines:

God is not in me, nor in you,

But between us.

God is not in me or mine, nor you or yours

But ours.

God is known not alone, but in relationship.

Not as separate lonely power, but through our kinship, our friendship,

through our healing and binding and raising up of each other.

To know God is to know others

to love God is to love others

to hear God is to hear others....[8]

EMPATHY

A genuine spiritual relationship requires empathy, which is the ability to feel another's needs and wants. "When we empathize," writes Robert L. Katz *(z"l)*, the late Professor of Human Relations at Hebrew Union College–Jewish Institute of Religion, "we take on the personality of another person and try out his experiences."[9] He goes on to say that there is a difference between empathy and sympathy. When we sympathize with another person, we are preoccupied with the assumed duality or the parallel between our feelings and the feelings of the other, whereas the empathizer tends to abandon self-consciousness. This can lead to self-transcendence, which is an important ingredient of spirituality.

Empathy and love are related, as is illustrated by the following story attributed to a Hasidic master, Rabbi Moshe Leib of Sasov:

> How I love men is something I learned from a peasant. He was sitting in an inn along with other peasants, drinking. For a long time he was as silent as all the rest, but when he was moved by the wine, he asked one of the men seated beside him: "Tell me, do you love me or don't you love me?" The other replied: "I love you very much." But the first peasant replied: "You say that you love me, but you do not know what I need. If you really loved me, you would know." The other had not a word to say to this, and the peasant who had put the question fell silent again.
>
> But I understood. To know the needs of men and to bear the burden of their sorrow—that is the true love of men.[10]

Every loving relationship involves empathy. In fact, there can be no love without empathy. For, as the psychiatrist and Jewish social philosopher Erich Fromm argued, love is the active concern for the life and the growth of the other. He wrote, "If I love the other person, I feel one with him or her, but with him *as he is*, not as I need him to be as an object for my use."[11]

By transcending the limits of our rational power and by extending ourselves to another person, we open ourselves to the possibility of spiritual awakening.

DEEDS OF LOVINGKINDNESS

How does one translate these sentiments of concern for the other into daily activities? We can find a possible answer in the Jewish concept of *gemilut hasadim,* often translated as "deeds of lovingkindness." This is a much wider and deeper than the idea of *tzedakah,* usually rendered as "charity" or "justice." As it is written in the Talmud,

> Charity is done only to the living, loving deeds also to the dead; charity is given only to the poor, loving deeds both to the rich and the poor; charity is given with money, loving deeds with money and with personal service. (Suk. 49b)

Elaborating on these differences, Rabbi David A. Cooper states, "In many ways, charity is simpler, cleaner, and easier than lovingkindness. Once we hand it over, we are done with it. However, there is never an end of lovingkindness." Interestingly, *gemilut hasadim* is also extended to animals. Jewish law has several requirements pertaining to the humane treatment of animals *(tzar baale hayyim),* such as the feeding of an animal before oneself, the obligation to relieve an animal of pain even on Shabbat, and the duty to slaughter an animal with as little suffering as possible.

By doing deeds of lovingkindness, an individual follows God's example. As the ancient sage taught us,

> "You shall walk after the Lord your God" (Deuteronomy 13:5). But how can a person walk after God who is "a devouring fire" (Deuteronomy 4:24)? It means, walk after the divine attributes: namely, clothe the naked, visit the sick, comfort the mourner, bury the dead. (Sot. 14a)

Every individual, therefore, is enjoined to carry out good deeds. Based on Deuteronomy 15:11, "You shall open your hand wide to your brother," one rabbinic source says,

> To him for whom bread is suitable, give bread; to him who needs dough, give dough; to him for whom money is required, give money; to whom for whom it is fitting to put the food in his mouth, put it in. (Sifre, Deut. Reeh, #118)

In his *Sefer Ma'alot Hamidot,* the thirteenth-century author Yechiel ben Yekutiel ben Benyamin Harofe Anav gives an extended list of a person's responsibilities in this area:

> And what is *gemilut chasadim?* That a person will be merciful, having compassion for others, just as God is merciful and full of compassion.... And a person should be kind to everyone—to the rich and to the poor, to the living and to the dead. And a person should draw the estranged near and the near even closer. If they need support, he should support them; if they need clothing, he should clothe them; if they need a place to stay, he should take them into his home; if they are in need of money, he should lend it to them; if they need to borrow an item, he should lend it to them; if they need to study Torah, he should teach it to them; if they need to be rebuked, he should rebuke them. He should speak well of them and ignore their blemishes. When they are happy, he should be happy with them. And when they are sad, he should cheer them up. When he sees a person wasting his possessions and denigrating himself, he should draw that person near to him and admonish him. Thus it is with everything that one sees in one's friend.... Therefore, my students, be careful and diligent with this important virtue in order that you will merit the presence of *Shechinah* [the Divine] and bask in its glow.[12]

Examples of *Gemilut Hasadim*

Many people devote their time and energy to doing good deeds. Some do this occasionally or even periodically, others actually devote the major part of their discretionary time to *gemilut hasadim*. They may or may not be active in their religious institutions, but they have chosen this spiritual path because of their willingness and ability to improve the lives of others.

In the *Hasidic Anthology* we find an example of such a loving act:

> Rabbi Hirsch Ziditzover narrated the following story: "Once when I was a disciple of the Sassover Rabbi, I wished to see the Rabbi's midnight service for the 'Exile of the *Shechinah.*' I concealed myself in his home, and at midnight, I saw the Rabbi arise from his bed, dress in peasant garments, take some logs of wood and an axe, and walk out of the house. I followed him in silence, and saw him step into a hut where a woman had given birth to a child a few days before. Her husband was not in the town, and no one had come to kindle a fire for her in the cold night. The Sassover said to her in Polish: 'Buy my wood very cheap; you may pay me later.' The woman replied: 'I have no strength to chop it and to light the fire.' 'I have an axe and will do it for you,' was the reply.
>
> "While chopping the wood, the Rabbi recited 'Tikkun Leah,' the first part of the service; and while making the fire, he said the 'Tikkun Rachel,' the balance of it. Then he returned to his home, changed his garments, and commenced his studies."[13]

In 1995, Aaron Feuerstein, a prominent industrialist in the greater Boston area, sustained a major fire in his textile factory. When his mill became inoperative, he refused to let go of his employees or cut their benefits. Since this tragedy occurred in the midst of winter, he promised them a month's pay, a Christmas bonus, and health coverage for three months. More importantly, he said he was determined to rebuild his business instead of retiring. This endeavor brought hope to hundreds of people who would have gone on welfare or suffered outright poverty. By this act, he won the accolades of thousands who admired his kindness for ignoring the "bottom line" thinking that predominates in the business community. He was recognized by President Clinton and mentioned in the State of the Union Address. When asked why he did such a praiseworthy thing, he attributed it to his religious upbringing and then quoted Hillel's teaching: "When people do not act as human beings, strive to be human" (Av. 2:6).

We have all known caring individuals who devote their lives to a variety of humanitarian causes, such as helping the poor, working with inner-city children, and comforting the sick and the needy. These people derive strength, personal satisfaction, and a sense of fulfillment as they go about helping others, at times under very difficult conditions. For them, aiding other human beings who are created in the "image of God" is of great religious value. They act in the spirit of the ancient rabbis who taught that "any person who saves the life of another individual, it is as if that person had saved the whole world" (San. 4:5). This is a major avenue of spirituality. Each act of lovingkindness brings blessings to others as it brings the person closer to God.

Dedication to a Jewish Cause

The passion for *gemilut hasadim* often leads people to dedicate themselves, totally or in large measure, to specific Jewish causes. Some people who are committed to Jewish continuity consider Jewish education their most cherished commitment. Others volunteer within Jewish communal organizations. There are those who give their all to medical institutions that save lives. These personal interests are often all-consuming and self-transcending. Here are three examples of such causes, from among many:

Zionism

Throughout Jewish history, there have been people who were fervently committed to the establishment and preservation of the Jewish state in Israel. After Theodor Herzl (1860–1904), the founder of modern political Zionism, many Jews took this as a major cause for themselves, spending a great deal of effort to spread the word about the need for a state in the land of our ancestors. They worked with local organizations, raised funds, set up meetings, and rallied Jews as well as non-Jews around the idea and ideal of Zionism.

Even though Israel has been now a reality since 1948, many Jews still devote themselves to Zionist causes, including Israel bonds and peace in the Middle East. For these individuals, Israel's survival and prosperity constitute an all-engulfing passion, providing a spiritual high that connects them to the people and land of Israel.

My experiences as a congregational rabbi in Buenos Aires, Argentina, from 1966 to 1969 left me with a strong impression that most South American Jews today identify with political Zionism as the predominant manifestation of their Jewishness. The percentage of Latin American Jews who belong to synagogues is considerably less than those who support the Zionist causes in Israel. I have met countless individuals there, as I do now in the United States, who are "burning with the love of Zion." Zionism is their main path to personal spirituality.

Worthy Social Causes

The term *tikkun olam* is mostly associated with Lurianic Kabbalah, and according to Gershom Scholem, means "the harmonious correction and mending of the flaw which came into the world."[14] It is, as we saw before, based on Luria's teachings that the universe emerged as a result of divine contraction *(tzimtzum)* and the consequent breaking of the vessels that could not absorb the divine light.

The hope for the future is that the sparks of light, which have spread out, will be once again gathered and brought into wholeness. This process of mending is called *tikkun olam* ("the mending of the universe"), and according to Luria, it is in the hands of every individual. In other words, by observing *mitzvot,* each of us can contribute to the restoration of the world. This places an enormous responsibility upon us. Consequently, if anyone refuses to do his or her part, it is as if that person is standing in the way of wholeness.

In our time, this concept has taken a specialized meaning: social action. Thus, prominent champions in this area, such as Rabbi David Saperstein, the director of the Social Action Center of Washington, and his coauthor Albert Vorspan, another prominent leader who was the director of the Commission on Social Action of the UAHC until his recent retirement, write,

> Jewish theology teaches us that, when God created the universe, one small part of creation was intentionally left undone. That part was social action! God gave to human beings alone the ability to understand the difference between right and wrong, to choose between good and evil, to love, to empathize, and to dream. Then God challenged us to use those tools to complete creation. By allowing us to be partners in completing the world, God has given to our lives destiny and purpose.[15]

Early Reform Jews in this country placed a high priority on social action, considering it one of the cornerstones of their religious expression. The Columbus Platform of 1937, for example, states clearly that

> Seeking God means to strive after holiness, righteousness and goodness.... Judaism seeks the attainment of a just society by

the application of its teachings to the economic order, to industry and commerce, and to national and international affairs.

The Centenary Perspective of 1976, on the other hand, recognizes the tension that exists between the universalistic and the particularistic tendencies in Judaism, and tries to establish a balance between them. It states,

> Early Reform Jews, newly admitted to general society and seeing in this the evidence of a growing universalism, regularly spoke of Jewish purpose in terms of Jewry's service to humanity…. Until the recent past our obligations to the Jewish people and to all humanity seemed congruent…. We must, however, confront them without abandoning either of our commitments…. Judaism calls us simultaneously to universal and particular obligations.

In the "Principles for Reform Judaism" (1999) we now have the widest expression of commitment to the betterment of society. We read,

> Partners with God in *tikkun olam,* repairing the world, we are called to help bring nearer the messianic age. We seek dialogue and joint action with people of other faiths in the hope that together we can bring peace, freedom and justice to our world. We are obligated to pursue *tzedek,* justice and righteousness, and to narrow the gap between the affluent and the poor, to act against discrimination and oppression, to pursue peace, to welcome the stranger, to protect the earth's biodiversity and natural resources, and to redeem those in physical, economic and spiritual bondage…. We affirm the *mitzvah* of *tzedakah,* setting aside portions of our earnings and our time to provide for those in need.

Across the United States, many synagogue movements today[16] still consider social action a major aspect of their community work. Inspired by the biblical teachings to "establish justice in the gate" (Amos 5:15) and to "uphold the rights of the orphan, defend the cause of the widow" (Isaiah 1:17) or to "seek peace and pursue it" (Psalms 34:15), congregants often commit themselves to making a serious difference in society. For example, they work in soup kitchens, volunteer to teach reading in inner-city communities, and defend the rights of migrant farm workers. They do all this and more because of their Jewish religious consciousness, not only because of their own good heart. There are yet others who are not formally affiliated with temples but still engage in these worthy activities because of their Jewish upbringing. For these individuals, doing good represents the highest level of religiosity and a primary pathway in their spiritual growth.

But is social action a "Jewish" cause? There is no doubt that historically, Jews have expressed concern for the well-being of their own people. They even considered the redemption of their own kind as one of the most important religious duties. According to the Jewish law,

> Ransoming captives (*pidyon shevuyyim*) comes before feeding and clothing the poor, because there is no greater *mitzvah* than to ransom captives. For whatever important purpose money may have been collected, it may be set aside in order to ransom captives, even money collected for the purpose of building a synagogue. (Yoreh Dea, #252)

But what about our responsibility to humanity at large? No one denies that our first responsibility is to our own, just as a family has a duty to preserve its members before doing anything for others. Yet, there are new voices that ask for a wider humanitarian concern. In a pamphlet issued by the Jewish Founders Network Tenth National Conference, the issue is framed as follows:

Some founders believe that we must focus our efforts on the needs of the Jewish community, building day schools and preserving Israel's water supply. Others argue that we have a responsibility to alleviate urban poverty in America and provide basic health care in Africa. Who decides whether we save an aging synagogue or an endangered species? Are these either/or choices?

Today, with more resources available to us, and following the teaching of those who encourage us to consider humanity as a whole, the need to widen the scope of social action and bring healing and hope to others who are in need becomes clear. In fact, the State of Israel has shown sensitivity to this issue and provided help to those suffering the ravaging results of war in the Balkans. As Rabbi Tirzah Firestone writes,

> As Jews, we are taught never to endanger life, but to sustain it at all costs. But it is not the case that Jews are interconnected only with Jews or that Jews are responsible for the land of Israel and no other parcel of earth. If we fail to care for one another and the earth that sustains us all, regardless of our nationhood, we simply will not continue as a human species. That includes Jews.[17]

The Religious Action Center in Washington, D.C., led by Rabbi David Saperstein, has fought for justice for all people around the globe. Here is an example, as told by Al Vorspan, director emeritus of the Commission on Social Action of Reform Judaism:

> A significant congressional force was going to approve the Wye package offering aid to Israel and the Palestinians to implement the peace process, but wanted to deny foreign aid to Africa and Latin America. Clinton threatened to veto the bill as narrow. Some pro-Israel advocates insisted we ally with the

"pro-Israel" forces in the Congress, and not gamble on the larger program. But not the Religious Action Center of Reform Judaism. We backed the president and demanded respect for our coalition partners and the needs of the larger world. And we prevailed.[18]

ECOLOGY

According to the rabbis, before the creation of this world, God went on creating others and destroying them, saying, "These [i.e., heaven and earth] please Me; those did not please Me" (Ber. R. 9:2). When the work of creation was completed, God then placed Adam in the Garden of Eden and asked him "to till it and tend it" (Genesis 2:15). The earth's preservation was now in his hand. Furthermore, as Rabbi Marcia Prager remarks, at the end of Creation, "God surveyed all that had been made, and declared creation to be 'very good.' Very good—but not perfect."[19]

Humanity is a copartner with God in the act of preservation of the world. In fact, the rabbis argued that Adam was created last in the process of creation so that "he might straightway go in to the banquet" (San. 38a, Soncino). In other words, his creation at the end was done in order for "all nature to be ready for his use." This the rabbis compare to a king who builds palaces and furnishes them, and at the end brings in the guests. Adam—and, by extension, all humanity—are guests on the face of the earth. We are expected to protect it and preserve it for the future generations.

The members of *Shomrei Adamah*,[20] the Keepers of the Earth, a Jewish organization established by Ellen Bernstein, are dedicated to the proposition that we are here to cultivate ecological thinking and practices that have been integral to Jewish thinking through the centuries. The Psalmist said, "The heavens are the heavens of the Lord; but the earth has He given to the chil-

dren of human beings" (Psalms 115:16). We are to be stewards of
the earth and caretakers of the environment. The earth is here
for our use, not abuse. One of the activists, Shira Dicker, wrote
a set of Thirteen Precepts, à la Maimonides, to emphasize this
point. Here are her "Thirteen Intimate Interactions with Nature
That Are Key to Our Spiritual Well-Being":

> I believe, with a deep and abiding faith, that it is a holy act to
> walk barefoot in the grass and occasionally roll down a soft
> grassy hill.
>
> I believe, with a deep and abiding faith, that it is a holy act to
> sleep outdoors, under the canopy of heaven.
>
> I believe, with a deep and abiding faith, that it is a holy act to
> watch the sun come up over the ocean.
>
> I believe, with a deep and abiding faith, that it is a holy act to
> bask in the healing rays of the sun.
>
> I believe, with a deep and abiding faith, that it is a holy act to
> stand in an open meadow on a clear, starry night.
>
> I believe, with a deep and abiding faith, that it is a holy act to
> climb a mountain.
>
> I believe, with a deep and abiding faith, that it is a holy act to
> sit among the branches of a tree.
>
> I believe, with a deep and abiding faith, that it is a holy act to
> swim in a lake or a river or an ocean or a bay and feel your
> body supported by water.
>
> I believe, with a deep and abiding faith, that it is a holy act to
> take a great gulp of country air by night or after rainfall.
>
> I believe, with a deep and abiding faith, that it is a holy act to
> jump into great piles of crunchy autumn leaves.

I believe, with a deep and abiding faith, that it is a holy act to build sandcastles and feel the sand run through your fingers and slip between your toes.

I believe, with a deep and abiding faith, that it is a holy act to plant vegetables and herbs or simply dig in dirt.

I believe, with a deep and abiding faith, that it is a holy act to dance barefoot in the moonlight, see the horizon, witness a rainbow, get grass stains on your shirts, smell a barnyard, ride a horse, milk a cow, pet a cat, hug a tree, touch the sky.[21]

Cherishing relationships with others, the practice of *gemilut hasadim,* and dedication to Jewish causes represent noteworthy paths of spirituality. Those who prefer to engage in these sacred endeavors bring blessings not only to themselves but also to those around them.

CHAPTER 9

Finding Your Spiritual Path

A s HUMAN BEINGS, we have limited knowledge and life spans. We also live in a universe that is as immense as it is mysterious. If, as Plato taught us, philosophy begins in wonder (Theatetus 155D), I agree with Rabbi Abraham Joshua Heschel when he says, "Religion begins with the sense of the ineffable."[1] What should be our response? Rabbi Heschel writes, "In the face of nature's grandeur and mystery we must respond with awe."[2] However, this sense of awe—what Heschel calls "a radical amazement"[3]—must lead to a personal philosophy as well as a mode of behavior. Thus, he adds, "The root of religion is the question what to do with the feeling for the mystery of living, what to do with awe, wonder or fear."[4] Therefore, it is not enough to express a sense of awe; one must also respond with a deliberate course of action. This can take various forms: taking note of acts of transcendence, offering an appropriate prayer, completing a ritual act, engaging in meditation, carrying out deeds of lovingkindness, or dedicating oneself to a discipline of study.

Each of these responses, as well as others like them, represents a Jewish path to knowing God. For me, all of them are spiritually legitimate. Our tradition provides us with appropriate vehicles to express our spirituality within the framework of Judaism. In this area, Jewish sages, taking into account the need and makeup of the individual Jew, have been very generous in outlining for us various alternatives. Some have answered more emotionally, others with their intellect. For some, ritual has been the appropriate medium, for others, the answer lies in mystical speculation. Still others have dedicated their lives to social action.

Having covered the basic six spiritual paths identified in this study, it is time now to encourage you, the reader, to discover or validate your own spiritual path or even to charter a new one for yourself. It is also appropriate for me to share my preferred route. Let me start with the second item.

MY QUEST

My quest for spirituality began when I was a little boy living in Istanbul, Turkey. Like many kids my age, I was sent to *mahazike hatorah* ("those who strengthen the Torah"), an Orthodox religious school, which was equivalent to an afternoon and weekend yeshivah. There I studied prayers and some rabbinic texts. I even became a *shohet* (ritual slaughterer). For many years I acted as a *hazzan kavua* (permanent cantor/reader), a designated cantor for our junior congregation.

But when I reached my teenage years and my curiosity increased, I started to ask questions about the nature of God and the authorship of many of the classic Hebrew texts. Finding my teachers' answers evasive and unsatisfactory, I turned to other Jewish sources, where I discovered multiple theological options. The search for meaning and purpose led me, after I had studied law at the University of Istanbul and served in the Turkish army, first to the Institut International d'Etudes Hebraiques in Paris, France, and then to Hebrew Union College–Jewish Institute of Religion in Cincinnati, Ohio. I received my ordination in 1966 and then served Reform Jewish congregations in Buenos Aires,

Argentina; in Philadelphia (during my doctoral studies at the University of Pennsylvania); in Glencoe, Ilinois; and now in Needham, Massachusetts.

By nature, I am an observer of human behavior and a rationalist who asks for verifiable evidence. I tend to look at issues from a critical and historical perspective. I have faith in human beings and easily empathize with their struggles. I have great reverence for life and its possibilities. Though aware of the unknown that surrounds us, I maintain that the more we learn, the more we discover the mysteries of nature. This search is exciting and illuminating. It has the tone of religious fervor.

Like many, I have had a long and winding spiritual search and traversed through many theological landscapes. My inquiries started, like those of many in my generation, within the context of classical theism, which views God as an all-powerful, all-knowing and all-good Supreme Being. This God is also a "personal God" who relates to you and me. Then I moved to limited theism wherein God has the same characteristics without being all-powerful. However, I found both these viewpoints wanting. They failed to explain to me the mystery of evil, the question of free will, and the role of prayer. I found mysticism unappealing and anti-intellectual (though I must admit that after doing a lot of reading on this subject, I am intrigued by some of its teachings). I toyed with Spinoza's philosophy of pantheism ("all is God") for a while but was not satisfied with his determinism. Humanism, with its belief that God is not a reality but simply an idea in our mind, left me uninspired. I simply can't relate to Buber and his God concept based on an I-Thou relationship. Thankfully, through Rabbis Roland Gittelsohn, Mordecai Kaplan, Levi Olan, and other religious naturalists, I discovered the reality of God as the power or energy of the universe. This approach met my needs and provided a positive framework for my religious yearnings.

When I look around me and observe the workings of the

world, I see order and harmony, and I assume, as the Greek philosophers of antiquity did, that this order implies an ordering mind, a God, who exists not only in our imagination but also as a reality within the universe. This divine power may or may not know me but certainly makes my life possible, and for this I am grateful. I believe the universal immanent energy called God functions through the laws of nature and does not willfully interfere in human affairs. I don't expect miracles, nor do I pray for them. And, if something goes wrong, and evil ensues, it is not because God willed it so but because we are still ignorant of all the mysteries of the universe.

For me, God energizes the universe from within and keeps an order observable in nature, such as the constant changes of seasons and the predictable trajectories of the stars. To this power we call God, I owe gratitude, not because God needs it but because we need to express thanks just for being who we are, and for the potential within us. My prayers, I maintain, change me more than they alter the course of nature. They are more in the mode of introspection or meditation as I try to "tap into" this ever-present energy named God. I affirm, as we saw in chapter 5, that "Who rise from prayer better persons, their prayer is answered."[5]

Within the context of my religious naturalism, my spirituality is expressed primarily through *talmud torah*, the study of Torah. On many occasions I have felt prayer comforting and sustaining. I have been energized by many transcendent moments that have blessed my life. I have also found meaning and purpose in carrying out good deeds. I cherish my relationships, with family and friends, and consider them sacred. I have also benefitted from the salutary results of meditation. Carrying out religious rituals always strengthens my sense of belonging to the Jewish people, and enables me to confirm the values underlying each act. Yet, the one activity that constantly fills me with joy is probing an ancient or a modern text, and obtaining new insights for understanding myself, my community, my people, and the world around me.

When I study a biblical text, a rabbinic commentary, or a Jewish historical account, either ancient or modern, I feel as if I am engaged in a deep spiritual exercise. I keep in mind the statement in *Seder Eliyahu Rabbah* that "The Holy One studies with him who studies alone" (ch. 18). And if I am able to extract a new insight from any of the traditional sources, I often exclaim, in the spirit of our ancestor Jacob: Surely God was here, and I have just discovered a new aspect of the world suffused by divinity.

I study Jewish classic texts looking for religious values by which to live. But I also believe in *torah lishmah* and pursue it for the sheer joy of it. In this respect, I much admire Spinoza, who long ago taught us that to really know is to know God. And to the extent that my studies lead me to some knowledge and understanding, and hopefully to a bit of wisdom, my spirituality is enhanced and my religious transcendence established.

FINDING YOUR PATH

Spirituality cannot be imposed. It has to be discovered by each discerning individual. This is a personal and a private matter. Your solution may represent a combination of a few alternatives. You may want to give priority to one path over another, or combine two of them. Spirituality is reflective of one's personality and inclination. As you become aware of your emotional and intellectual needs, and search for an appropriate path to meet them with integrity, you will soon realize that you have a preference for certain paths among the many.

But that is only a beginning. A spiritual quest requires expending some effort. Not only must you be sensitive to your own needs, but having discovered your own spiritual niche, you must now also be willing to work on it. You need to practice meditation, or you must dedicate time and energy to carrying out good deeds, or you must set aside specific hours for study. You may wish to combine some of these paths or go from one to another. Whatever you decide, you need to keep in mind that your chosen activity must be carried out on a regular basis, very much as a way of life. Once you find your own spiritual path, that will become your life. It may lead you to other endeavors, to other means of exploration, but the dominant route will stay with you.

Your spiritual search will most likely lead you to others who share your point of view. This may even help you understand the issues better from this particular perspective. If you are Jewish, your spiritual path and the others you meet will bring you closer not only to the spirituality of Judaism but also to the practice of our religion. Discover the beauty of Shabbat and holy days, the inspiring rituals that stand for cherished values, the uplifting influence of regular prayers, the heartwarming feeling of doing something good for your fellow human beings. Affiliate with a synagogue and support its programs. Identify with a Jewish cause and get personally involved in it. If you prefer a more solitary act, such as meditation, remember that even this personal discipline must lead to *tikkun olam,* the betterment of our world. Ultimately, become aware of the beauty around you, of moments of insight and transcendence, and remember that it all comes from the Source of all Life.

However, as you settle in your spiritual path, I hope you will admit, both intellectually and emotionally, that your way is not the only legitimate way, even though it may be the best one for you. I hope you will be open to other alternatives as you mature and deepen your understanding of life and its challenges.

Orthodox Jews assume that Torah contains all the wisdom in the world, and all we have to do is search for it, either through the plain meaning of the text or by means of reinterpretation. "Turn [the Torah] over and over," taught Ben Bag Bag, "for it contains everything" (Av. 5:25). Liberal Jews, on the other hand, look at Torah in a more linear way as a main source of wisdom, maintaining that some of the teachings cannot be sustained now (such as slavery, killing witches, and discrimination against women). They look for insights that come from the inspiring teachers of all times, blending them within a Jewish context. The old *Union Prayer Book* of the Reform movement contains a prayer dealing with this matter. It reads: "O Lord, open our eyes that we may see and welcome all truth, whether shining from the annals of ancient revelations or teaching us through the seers of our time; for Thou hidest not Thy light from any generation of Thy children that yearn for Thee and seek Thy guidance."[6]

The challenge of finding your path is an exciting one, no matter how difficult it might be. But the rewards are plentiful. Finding and following your path not only will open a window through which you will see the world with a sense of awe and reverence but also will help you reach wholeness in your life. Not necessarily happiness or fortune, mind you, but a better understanding of your position in life, a greater appreciation for what you have and are, a contentment based on gratitude, and hopefully a desire to make things better for others. And this is nothing short of living in the presence of the God, the Source of all Life.

Abbreviations

Av.	Avot	NJPS	New (translation) JPS
BB	Babba Batra	Pes. K.	Pesikta Kahana
BR	Bible Review	Pes. R.	Pesikta Rabbati
Ber.	Berakhot	R. H.	Rosh Hashanah
Ber. R.	Bereshit Rabba	RSV	Revised Standard Version
Deut. R.	Deuteronomy Rabba		(The New Oxford Bible)
Eccles. R.	Ecclesiastes Rabba	Shab.	Shabbat
Erub.	Erubin	San.	Sanhedrin
Ex. R.	Exodus Rabba	S.H.	Shulchan Arukh
Gen. R.	Genesis Rabba	S. of S. R.	Song of Songs Rabba
Hag.	Hagigah	Sot.	Sotah
J	Jerusalem	Suk.	Sukkah
J. Ber.	Jerusalem Berakhot	Ta.	Ta'anit
Kid.	Kiddushin	Tanh.	Tanhumah
Lev. R.	Leviticus Rabba	Tanh. B.	Tanhumah
Men.	Menahot		(Buber's Edition)
Meg.	Megillah	Tem.	Temurot
Mek.	Mekilta	*z"l*	zikhrono livrakhah ("May
Naz.	Nazir		his memory be a blessing")
Ned.	Nedarim		

Notes

INTRODUCTION

1.   Erich Fromm, *Psychoanalysis and Religion* (New Haven, Conn.: Yale, 1958), 21.

CHAPTER 1

1.   Niles E. Goldstein, "The Spirituality of Shame," *Sh'ma* 28/554 (May 15, 1998).
2.   Michael Lerner, *Jewish Renewal* (New York: Putnam, 1994), xvii.
3.   Green, *Restoring the Aleph: Judaism for the Contemporary Seeker*, Council for Initiatives in Jewish Education Essay Series (1996): 11.
4.   Bill McKibben, "JoysRUs," *Utne Reader* (March/April 2000): 64.
5.   Quoted by Sara Isaacson, *Principles of Jewish Spirituality* (London: Thornsons, 1999), ix.
6.   David S. Ariel, *Spiritual Judaism* (New York: Hyperion, 1998), 2.
7.   See the article "The New Believers," *The Jerusalem Report* (April 2, 1998): 14–16.
8.   Karyn D. Kedar, *God Whispers: Stories of the Soul, Lessons of the Heart* (Woodstock, Vt.: Jewish Lights, 1999), 86.
9.   Green, op. cit., 5.

10. Harry Essrig, "Sichat Chulin," *The American Rabbi* 24/6 (June 1992): 2; See also his remarks in op. cit., 27/2, (October 1994): 42.
11. Francine Klagsbrun, "Feminine Spirituality," *Moment* (Aug. 1992): 12.
12. Harold L. Gelfman, *Central Conference of American Rabbis Newsletter* (May, 1998): 9.
13. Idem.
14. Charles S. Liebman, "When Prayer Becomes Leisure," *Forward* (June 11, 1999).
15. Michael Chernick, "Spirituality and Danger," in *Paths of Faithfulness*, ed. Carol Ochs, Kerry M. Olitzky and Joshua Saltzman (New York: KTAV, 1999), 20.
16. See the article by Neil Gillman "Judaism and the Search for Spirituality," *Conservative Judaism* (Winter 1985/86): 5.
17. Jeffrey J. Weisblatt, "Spirituality," *The American Rabbi* (October 1993): 9.
18. Martin A. Cohen, "What is Jewish Spirituality?" in *Paths of Faithfulness*, 28.
19. Roland B. Gittelsohn, *Wings of the Morning* (New York: Union of American Hebrew Congregations, 1969), 90.
20. Nancy Fuchs-Kreimer, *Sh'ma* 27/522 (November 29, 1996): 6.
21. Arthur Green, ed., *Jewish Spirituality from the Bible through the Middle Ages* (New York: Crossroad, 1987), xiii ff.
22. Deanne H. Shapiro, Jr. and Johanna Shapiro, "Spirituality in Reform Judaism," *Jewish Spectator* (Winter 1992): 32.
23. Lawrence Kushner, "Facing the Unity of God," *Tikkun* (May/June 1992): 53. Also, "Spirituality Is That Dimension of Living in Which We Are Aware of God's Presence," *Eyes Remade for Wonder: A Lawrence Kushner Reader* (Woodstock, Vt.: Jewish Lights, 1998), 12; "Spirituality Is Personal Immediacy and the Immediacy of God's Presence," ibid., 153.
24. Weisblatt, op. cit., 9.
25. Kerry M. Olitzky, "Toward a Personal Definition of Jewish Spirituality," in *Paths of Faithfulness*, 113.
26. Ariel, op. cit., 5. See others in the popular *Hadassah Magazine* (November 1996).

27. For further exploration of the idea of the quest for meaning in life, see Viktor Frankl, *Man's Search for Meaning* (New York: Washington Square Press, 1985).

28. All biblical translations are taken from *Tanakh—The Holy Scriptures* (Philadelphia: Jewish Publication Society, 1985).

29. Moses Maimonides, *The Guide of the Perplexed*, trans. S. Pines (Chicago: University of Chicago Press, 1963), I:40, 90.

30. Gershom Scholem, *Kabbalah* (New York: Meridian, 1978), 155. See also William Blank, *Torah, Tarot and Tantra* (Boston: Coventure, 1991), 37.

31. Blank, op. cit., 37.

32. Wayne Dosick, *Soul Judaism: Dancing with God into a New Era* (Woodstock, Vt.: Jewish Lights, 1997), 67–68.

33. Neil Gillman, *Sh'ma* (November 29, 1996), 5.

34. Mindy A. Portnoy argues that there are three complementary aspects of Jewish spirituality: (1) Study, (2) Ritual, and (3) Community. See "Spirituality," *The American Rabbi* 27/4 (February 1995), 17–24.

CHAPTER 2

1. Helmer Ringgren, *Israelite Religion* (Philadelphia: Fortress, 1963), 122, (quoting Pedersen).

2. E.E. Urbach, *The Sages* (Cambridge, Mass.: Harvard University Press, 1979), 214.

3. An echo of this meaning is found even in some of the rabbinic texts, as for example: "Rabbi Meir went to intercalate the year in Asya and there was no Megillah [the Scroll of Esther] there, and he wrote one out by heart *(milibo)* and read it" (Meg. 18b).

4. *The Anchor Bible Dictionary* (New York: Doubleday, 1992), Vol. 4, 376.

5. Jeffrey H. Tigay, *JPS Torah Commentary—Deuteronomy* (Philadelphia: Jewish Publication Society, 1996), 77.

6. *Ancient Near Eastern Texts*, 537, #24.

7. The origins of the synagogue, the bastion of rabbinic power, are obscure. Though a few sources ascribe its origin to Moses, tradition claims that it was established by the exilic Jews in Babylon and

brought back to Israel with the returnees. The Talmud, in fact, ascribes the formulation of the earliest prayers to be recited in the synagogue to Ezra and his successors (Ber. 33a). However, we have archaeological evidence that synagogues already existed in Egypt as early as the third century B.C.E. Recently, it was discovered that synagogues existed while the Second Temple still stood.

8. Robert Goldenberg, "Law and Spirit in Talmudic Religion," in *Jewish Spirituality from the Bible through the Middle Ages*, ed. Arthur Green (New York: Crossroad, 1987), 246.

9. Ibid., 249.

10. For different meanings of the term *mitzvah* in the Reform movement, see *Gates of Mitzvah*, ed. Simeon J. Maslin (New York: Central Conference of American Rabbis, 1979), 97–115.

11. J. Albo, *Book of Principles*, ed. I. Husic (Philadelphia: Jewish Publication Society, 1946), I:21, 173.

12. Louis Jacobs, *Jewish Theology* (West Orange, N.J.: Behrman, 1973), 156.

13. For more detail, see Shlomo Pines, "*Al ha-munah 'ruhaniyut' umeqorav ve-al mishnato shel Yehuda Halevi*," *Tarbitz* (July/September 1988): 511ff. (Hebrew).

14. Martin Buber, *Tales of the Hasidim: The Early Masters* (New York: Schocken, 1961), 58.

15. Ibid., 48.

16. Quoted in Louis Jacobs, *Hasidic Thought* (West Orange, N.J.: Behrman, 1976), 95.

17. Idem.

18. Gershom Scholem, *Kabbalah* (New York: Meridian, 1978), 160.

19. Jacobs, *Hasidic Thought*, op. cit., 63.

20. Idem.

21. Tamar Frankiel and Judy Greenfeld, *Minding the Temple of the Soul: Balancing Body, Mind, and Spirit through Traditional Jewish Prayer, Movement, and Meditation* (Woodstock, Vt.: Jewish Lights, 1997), 19.

22. For various God concepts in Judaism, see, among others, Rifat Sonsino and Daniel B. Syme, *Finding God* (New York: Union of American Hebrew Congregations, 1986) (reprinted by Northvale, N.J.:

Jason Aronson, 1993); *God in the Teachings of Conservative Judaism*, ed. S. Siegel and E. Gertel (New York: Rabbinical Assembly, 1985).

CHAPTER 3

1. Helmer Ringgren, *Israelite Religion* (Philadelphia: Fortress, 1963), 91.
2. Moses Maimonides, *The Guide of the Perplexed*, trans. S. Pines (Chicago: University of Chicago Press, 1963), I:64, 157.
3. Ibid., I/4, 28.
4. In the Bible, many people claim to have "seen" God (see, for example, Exodus 24:11; I Kings 22:19; Isaiah 6:1; Ezekiel 1:26), but no description is ever given.
5. There is a question in this text regarding the relationship between God's "goodness" and "presence." Upon closer examination, we note that God promises to let the divine "goodness" pass before Moses. This, however, is later identified with divine "presence" in v. 22. This means that at times, divine *kavod* is defined in terms of God's compassionate acts of mercy and kindness, namely, God's *tuv* (as in v. 19).
6. For a short biography, see Gershom Scholem, *Encyclopaedia Judaica*, Vol. 12, 861–866.
7. Martin Buber, *I and Thou*, trans. Ronald Gregor Smith (New York: Scribner's, 1958), 11.
8. Martin Buber, *Between Man and Man*, trans. Ronald Gregor Smith (New York: Macmillan, 1965), 22–23.
9. Ellen Bernstein, ed., *Ecology & the Jewish Spirit: Where Nature and the Sacred Meet* (Woodstock, Vt.: Jewish Lights, 1998), 18.
10. Ibid., 51.
11. Tirzah Firestone, *With Roots in Heaven* (New York: Dutton, 1998), 209–210.
12. Terry A. Bookman, "The Circuitous Path," in *Jewish Spiritual Journeys*, ed. Lawrence A. Hoffman and Arnold J. Wolf (West Orange, N.J.: Behrman, 1997), 142.
13. Glasberg, personal communication.
14. David A. Cooper, *Entering the Sacred Mountain* (New York: Bell Tower, 1994), 117–8 (o.p.) Rev. ed.: *The Handbook of Jewish Meditation*

Practices: A Guide for Enriching the Sabbath and Other Days of Your Life (Woodstock, Vt.: Jewish Lights), 2000.

15. Beth Moskowitz, "From the Temple President," Temple Aliyah, *Shofar* (Needham, Mass.: June 2000): 1.

16. Linda Sacks, "A God of Small Things," *Moment* (April 2000): 49.

17. Daniel B. Syme, personal communication.

18. Sheldon H. Blank, *Jeremiah* (Cincinnati: Hebrew Union College, 1961), 70.

19. Rabbi Meir ibn Gabbai, *Avodat Ha-Kodesh* (Jerusalem: 1973), *Ha-Takhlit*.

20. W. Gunther Plaut, *The Growth of Reform Judaism* (New York: World Union for Progressive Judaism, 1965), 97.

21. Buber, *Between Man and Man*, 23.

22. Buber, *I and Thou*, 115.

CHAPTER 4

1. For the differences between almsgiving and *gemilut hasadim*, Suk. 49b.

2. Where this teaching took place is not known, for the Bible does not make any reference to a "school." The first clear mention of a "school" is by Ben Sira (51: 23) in the post-biblical period. Scribal academies were known in Egypt and Mesopotamia as well as Canaan. It is highly unlikely that there were no schools in ancient Israel. For further details, see Rifat Sonsino, *Motive Clauses in Hebrew Law*, SBL Dissertation Series 45 (Chico, Calif.: Scholars Press, 1980), 130.

3. *Sefer Hahinukh* (The Book of [Mitzvah] Education), trans. Charles Wengrov (Jerusalem/New York: Feldheim, 1992), Vol. 4, p. 255 (No. 419).

4. Ibid., 257.

5. *The Book of Legends—Sefer Ha-Aggadah*, ed. Hayim N. Bialik and Yehoshua H. Ravnitsky, trans. William Braude (New York: Schocken, 1992). Henceforth, *Legends*.

6. Ibid., 261.

7. Idem.

8. Idem.

9. Moses Maimonides, *The Guide of the Perplexed*, trans. Shlomo Pines (Chicago: University of Chicago Press, 1963), III:54, 636.

10. Sheldon H. Blank, *Prophetic Faith in Isaiah* (New York: Harper, 1958), 140.

11. *Guide* 3/54, 637.

12. Ibid., 637–638.

13. Isadore Twersky, ed., *A Maimonides Reader* (West Orange, N.J.: Behrman, 1972), 419.

14. David Wolpe, *Teaching Your Children about God* (New York: Harper, 1995).

15. Susie Schneider, "Study as Meditation," in *Meditation from the Heart of Judaism: Today's Teachers Share Their Practices, Techniques, and Faith*, ed. Avram Davis (Woodstock, Vt.: Jewish Lights, 1999), 56.

16. Carol Ochs and Kerry M. Olitzky, *Jewish Spiritual Guidance* (San Francisco: Jossey-Bass, 1997), 121.

17. Lawrence Kushner, *Eyes Remade for Wonder: A Lawrence Kushner Reader* (Woodstock, Vt.: Jewish Lights, 1998), 33.

18. David Hartman, *A Heart of Many Rooms: Celebrating the Many Voices within Judaism* (Woodstock, Vt.: Jewish Lights, 1999), 47.

19. David A. Cooper, *God Is a Verb* (New York: Riverhead, 1997), 185.

20. Norman J. Cohen, "*Etz Hayyim Hi:* It Is a Tree of Life," in *Paths of Faithfulness* 42–43.

21. A. Stanley Dreyfus, "Random Observations on Spirituality," ed. Ochs, Olitzky, and Saltzman, in *Paths of Faithfulness*, 56.

22. Francine Klagsbrun, "Feminine Spirituality," *Moment* (August 1992), 17.

23. Bohnen, personal communication.

CHAPTER 5

1. See, for example, Isaiah 1:15.

2. See *Ancient Near Eastern Texts*, 365–401.

3. See, for example, Genesis 24:12–14; Numbers 12:13; Joshua 7:6–9; I Samuel 2:2–10; II Kings 19:15–19.

4. For a short history of liturgy, see *Encyclopaedia Judaica* Vol. 11, 392ff.

5. Harold Kushner, *Who Needs God?* (New York: Summit Books, 1989), 148.

6. Burt Jacobson, "Spiritual Centering," in *Worlds of Jewish Prayer*, ed. Shonahan Harris Wiener and Jonathan Omer-Man. (Northvale, N.J.: Jason Aronson, 1993), 7.

7. See, among others, Larry Dossey and Larry Vandecreek, eds., *Scientific and Pastoral Perspectives on Intercessory Prayer: An Exchange between Larry Dossey, M.D., and Health Care Chaplains* (Binghamton, N.Y.: Haworth Press, 1998); Reginald B. Cherry, M.D., *Healing Prayer: God's Divine Intervention in Medicine, Faith and Prayer* (Nashville, Tenn.: Thomas Nelson, 1999); Jessica Cohen, "Healing is Believing. Conventional Medicine Discovers the Power of Prayer." *Utne Reader* (March/April 2000), 20–22.

8. Abraham Joshua Heschel, *Man's Quest for God* (New York: Scribner's, 1954), 5.

9. Tamar Frankiel and Judy Greenfeld, *Minding the Temple of the Soul: Balancing Body, Mind, and Spirit through Traditional Jewish Prayer, Movement, and Meditation* (Woodstock, Vt.: Jewish Lights, 1997), 88.

10. Harold Kushner, *When Children Ask About God* (New York: Schocken, 1976), 157; see also Louis Jacobs, *A Jewish Theology* (West Orange, N.J.: Behrman, 1973), 187.

11. Moshe Greenberg, "On the Refinement of the Conception of Prayer in Hebrew Scriptures," *Association for Jewish Studies Review* I (1976): 84.

12. Ibid., 86.

13. Louis Jacobs, *A Jewish Theology*, 187.

14. Steinberg, *Basic Judaisms* 117.

15. Ochs and Olitzky, *Jewish Spiritual Guidance*, 40–45.

16. Lawrence A. Hoffman: *My People's Prayer Book*, Vol. 3 *P'sukei D'zimrah* (Woodstock, Vt.: Jewish Lights, 1999), 67.

17. *Guide*, 3:51.

18. Heschel, *Man's Quest for God*, 58.

19. Mordecai Kaplan, *The Meaning of God in Modern Jewish Religion* (New York: Jewish Reconstructionist Press, 1962), 33.

20. Rabbi Eric H. Yoffie. "Remarks to the UAHC Executive Committee" (New York: Union of American Hebrew Congregations, February 7, 2000), 3.
21. Marcia Prager, *The Path of Blessing* (New York: Bell Tower, 1998), 4.
22. Kushner, *When Children Ask About God*, 161.
23. *Gates of Prayer*, 157.
24. Ibid., 3.
25. Sheldon Zimmerman, *Healing of Soul, Healing of Body: Spiritual Leaders Unfold the Strength & Solace in Psalms*, ed. Simkha Y. Weintraub (Woodstock, Vt.: Jewish Lights, 1994), 101–102.
26. Shoni Labowitz, "Prayer as Ecstasy and Art," in *Worlds of Jewish Prayer*, ed. J. Omer-Man, 48.
27. Gershon Winkler, "Davvening on a Prayer," *Worlds of Jewish Prayer*, op. cit., 19–20.
28. Gittelsohn, personal communication.
29. Roland B. Gittelsohn, *Wings of the Morning* (New York: Union of American Hebrew Congregations, 1969), 132.
30. Roland B. Gittelsohn, "A Naturalist View," in *The Theological Foundations of Prayer*, ed. Jack Bemporad (New York: Union of American Hebrew Congregations, 1967), 46.
31. Idem.
32. Gittelsohn, *Wings of the Morning*, 152.
33. Ibid., 292.
34. Alan Lew, "Prayer and the Uses of Meditation," *Judaism* (Winter 2000): 94.
35. Samuel Kunin, "Silent Prayer," *Berit Mila Newsletter* 4, no.1 (May 25, 1992), 2.
36. John Gray, *I and II Kings: A Commentary* (Philadelphia: Westminster Press, 1970), 406.
37. *Jewish Advocate*, Boston, 8/19–25, 1994.
38. Rolando Matalon, personal communication.

CHAPTER 6

1. See Nahum Sarna, *The JPS Commentary—Genesis* (Philadelphia: Jewish Publication Society, 1989), 169, n. 63

2. David Winston, "Philo and the Contemplative Life," in *Jewish Spirituality*, ed. Arthur Green (New York: Crossroad, 1987), 219.

3. Gershom Scholem, "Meditation," *Encyclopaedia Judaica*, vol. 11, 1217.

4. Aryeh Kaplan, *Jewish Meditation* (New York: Schocken, 1985), 101.

5. Scholem, op. cit., 1217.

6. Avram Davis, ed., *Meditation from the Heart of Judaism: Today's Teachers Share Their Practices, Techniques, and Faith* (Woodstock, Vt.: Jewish Lights, 1999), 9. Cited as *Meditation* (Davis) in following notes.

7. Nan Fink Gefen, *Discovering Jewish Meditation: Instruction & Guidance for Learning an Ancient Spiritual Practice* (Woodstock, Vt.: Jewish Lights, 1999), 13.

8. See Sylvia Boorstein, *That's Funny, You Don't Look Buddhist: On Being a Faithful Jew and a Passionate Buddhist* (San Francisco: Harper San Francisco, 1996).

9. Lawrence Kushner, *Invisible Lines of Connection: Sacred Stories of the Ordinary* (Woodstock, Vt.: Jewish Lights, 1996), 121.

10. Rabbi James L. Mirel and Karen Bonnell Werth, *Stepping Stones to Jewish Spiritual Living: Walking the Path Morning, Noon, and Night* (Woodstock, Vt.: Jewish Lights, 1998), xix.

11. David Zeller, "A Splendid Way to Live," in *Meditation* (Davis), 112.

12. Kaplan, op. cit., 3.

13. Alan Lew, "It Doesn't Matter What You Call It: If It Works, It Works," in *Meditation* (Davis), 51.

14. Gefen, *Discovering Jewish Meditation*, 5.

15. Kaplan, op. cit., 49.

16. Scholem, op. cit., 1217.

17. Kaplan, op. cit., 51.

18. Mirel and Werth, op. cit., 18.

19. Kaplan, op. cit., 52.

20. Gefen, op. cit., 33.

21. Scholem, op. cit., 1219.

22. For an example, see Gefen, op. cit., 103.

23. Scholem, op. cit., 1218.

24. Kaplan, op. cit., 94f.

25. Blank, *Torah, Tarot and Tantra*, 149.

26. Ibid., 148.

27. Gefen, op. cit., 160.

28. Steven A. Moss, "Finding Spirituality through Meditation," *CCAR Journal* (Fall 1992): 47.

29. Gefen, op. cit., x.

30. Mindy Ribner, "Keeping God Before Me," in *Meditation* (Davis), 63.

31. Avram Davis, *Meditation* (Davis), 12.

32. Steve Fisdel, "Meditation as Our Own Jacob's Ladder," in *Meditation* (Davis), 120.

33. Avram Davis, The *Way of Flame: A Guide to the Forgotten Mystical Tradition of Jewish Meditation* (Woodstock, Vt.: Jewish Lights, 1999), 25–26.

34. Blank, op. cit., 147–161.

35. Lew, in *Meditation* (Davis), 46.

36. Daniel C. Matt, *God & the Big Bang: Discovering Harmony Between Science & Spirituality* (Woodstock, Vt.: Jewish Lights, 1996), 40.

37. Davis, *Meditation* (Davis),85.

38. Gefen, op. cit., 41ff.

39. Sylvia Boorstein, op. cit., 53.

40. Ibid., 219.

41. Mirel and Werth, op. cit., 18.

42. Gefen, op. cit., 83–84.

43. Tamar Frankiel and Judy Greenfeld, *Minding the Temple of the Soul: Balancing Body, Mind, and Spirit through Traditional Jewish Prayer, Movement, and Meditation* (Woodstock, Vt.: Jewish Lights, 1997), 122.

44. Abraham Abulafia, quoted by Daniel C. Matt, *The Essential Kabbalah* (Edison, N.J.: Castle Books, 1997), 103.

45. Blank, op. cit., 160.

46. Rami M. Shapiro, *Minyan* (New York: Bell Tower, 1997), 67.

47. Ibid., 73.

48. David A. Cooper, *Renewing Your Soul* (New York: Harper, 1995), 32 (o.p.) Rev. ed.: *The Handbook of Jewish Meditation Practices: A Guide for Enriching the Sabbath and Other Days of Your Life* (Woodstock, Vt.: Jewish Lights), 2000.

49. Kaplan, op. cit., 96.
50. Shapiro, op. cit., 63.
51. Fisdel, in *Meditation* (Davis), 122.
52. Davis, *Meditation* (Davis), 11.
53. Blank, op. cit., 150.
54. Frankiel and Greenfeld, op. cit., 22/23.
55. Gefen, op. cit., 19–20.
56. Moss, op. cit., 48.
57. Omer-Man, "Noble Boredom," in *Meditation* (Davis), 76–81.
58. David A. Cooper, *Entering the Sacred Mountain* (New York: Bell Tower, 1994), 82 (o.p.) Rev. ed.: *Three Gates to Meditation Practice: A Personal Journey into Sufism, Buddhism, and Judaism* (Woodstock, Vt.: SkyLight Paths), 2000.
59. Kennard Lipman, "On 'Meditation,'" *CCAR Journal* (Fall 1999): 26.
60. Zeller, in *Meditation* (Davis), 113.

CHAPTER 7

1. See, for example, Psalms 81:4.
2. Wayne Dosick, *Soul Judaism: Dancing with God into a New Era* (Woodstock, Vt.: Jewish Lights, 1997), 88.
3. Morris N. Kertzer, *What Is a Jew?* rev. Lawrence A. Hoffman (New York: Macmillan, 1993), 66.
4. Arthur Waskow, *Godwrestling—Round 2: Ancient Wisdom, Future Paths* (Woodstock, Vt.: Jewish Lights, 1996), 316.
5. Idem.
6. Tamar Frankiel and Judy Greenfeld, *Minding the Temple of the Soul: Balancing Body, Mind, and Spirit through Traditional Jewish Prayer, Movement, and Meditation* (Woodstock, Vt.: Jewish Lights, 1997), 126.
7. For different interpretations of *mitzvah* in Reform Judaism, see Simeon J. Maslin, ed., *Gates of Mitzvah* (New York: Central Conference of American Rabbis, 1979), 97–115.
8. On these clauses, see Rifat Sonsino, *Motive Clauses in Hebrew Law.* SBL Dissertation Series 45 (Chico, Calif.: Scholars Press, 1980).
9. Michael Strassfeld, *The Jewish Holidays* (New York: Harper, 1985), 80.

10. Avram Davis, *The Way of Flame: A Guide to the Forgotten Mystical Tradition of Jewish Meditation* (Woodstock, Vt.: Jewish Lights, 1999), 26.

11. Michael Lerner, *Jewish Renewal* (New York: Putnam, 1994), 295.

12. Joseph Telushkin, *Jewish Literacy* (New York: William Morrow, 1991), 495.

13. Louis Jacobs, *A Jewish Theology* (West Orange, N.J.: Behrman, 1973), 226–230.

14. Chaim Stern, ed., *On the Doorpost of Your House—Prayers and Ceremonies for the Jewish Home* (New York: Central Conference of American Rabis, 1994).

15. Francine Klagsbrun, "As Reform Turns Traditional," *Moment* (April 2000), 39.

16. See, for example, Leviticus 11 and *Kitzur Shulhan Arukh*, "Prohibited Foods," vol. 1, ch. 46.

17. Arthur Green, *These Are the Words: A Vocabulary of Jewish Spiritual Life* (Woodstock, Vt.: Jewish Lights, 1999), 94. See also Michael Lerner, *Jewish Renewal*, and Rabbi Rami M. Shapiro, *Minyan* (New York: Bell Tower, 1997), 145f. On Eco-Judaism, see *Torah of the Earth: Exploring 4,000 Years of Ecology in Jewish Thought, Vol. 2— Zionism: One Land, Two Peoples, Eco-Judaism: One Earth, Many Peoples*, ed. Arthur Waskow (Woodstock, Vt.: Jewish Lights, 2000).

18. Firestone, *With Roots in Heaven*, 257.

19. However, on the eve of Sabbath, one lights the candles and then recites the blessing. See Peter S. Knobel, ed., *The Gates of the Seasons* (New York: Central Conference of American Rabbis, 1983), 115.

20. Louis Jacobs, *The Book of Jewish Belief* (West Orange, N.J.: Behrman, 1984), 115.

21. Lawrence A. Hoffman, "Ritual, God and Me," in *Jewish Spiritual Journeys*, ed. Lawrence A. Hoffman and Arnold Wolf (West Orange, N.J.: Behrman, 1997), 45.

22. On the breaking of glass, see *Gates of Mitzvah*, 80–81.

23. Morris N. Kertzer, op. cit., 66.

24. Milton Steinberg, *Basic Judaism* (New York: Harcourt, Brace and World, 1947), 136.

25. Ron Wolfson, "My Top Ten Teaching Techniques," *Sh'ma* 24/462 (November 26, 1993): 4.

26. Jacob Neusner, "Why I Am Not an Ethnic Jew, Why I Am a Religious Jew," *Jewish Spectator* (Winter 1996/7), 16.

27. Marcia Prager, *The Path of Blessing* (New York: Bell Tower. 1998), 151.

CHAPTER 8

1. Michael Lerner, *Jewish Renewal* (New York: Putnam, 1994), 29.

2. Martin Buber, *Between Man and Man*, trans. R. G. Smith (New York: Macmillan, 1965), 19.

3. Martin Buber, *I and Thou*, trans. Walter Kaufmann (New York: Scribner's, 1970), 150.

4. Ibid., 151.

5. Ibid., 158.

6. Idem.

7. Menitoff, personal communication.

8. Harold Schulweis, "Between," in *Passages in Poetry* (Encino, Calif.: Valley Beth Shalom, 1990), 8.

9. Robert L. Katz, *Empathy* (Glencoe, Ill.: Free Press, 1963), 10.

10. Martin Buber, *Tales of the Hasidim: The Later Masters* (New York: Schocken, 1948), 86.

11. Erich Fromm, *The Art of Loving* (New York: Harper, 1956), 28.

12. Niles E. Goldstein and Steven S. Mason, *Judaism and Spiritual Ethics* (New York: Union of American Hebrew Congregations, 1996), 11–12.

13. Louis I. Newman, *Hasidic Anthology* (New York: Schocken, 1975), 209. This is the basis of the famous story "If Not Higher" by I. L. Peretz. See his *Selected Stories* (New York: Schocken, 1975), 38–40.

14. Gershom Scholem, *On the Kabbalah and Its Symbolism* (New York: Schocken, 1965), 110.

15. Albert Vorspan and David Saperstein, *Tough Choices* (New York: Union of American Hebrew Congregations, 1992), 6.

16. For statements on this subject by the Conservative movement in

Judaism, see *Emet Ve-Emunah—Statement of Principles of Conservative Judaism* (New York: Jewish Theological Seminary, 1988), 45; "'You Shall Strengthen Them' (Leviticus 25:35)—A Rabbinic Letter on the Poor" (New York: The Rabbinical Assembly, 1999).

17. Tirzah Firestone, *With Roots in Heaven* (New York: Dutton, 1998), 333.

18. Al Vorspan, "The Jacques Attack," *Reform Judaism* (Spring 2000): 16.

19. Marcia Prager, *The Path of Blessing*, 56.

20. See Ellen Bernstein's book *Ecology & the Jewish Spirit: Where Nature and the Sacred Meet* (Woodstock, Vt.: Jewish Lights, 1998).

21. Ibid., 212–123.

CHAPTER 9

1. Abraham Joshua Heschel, *Man Is Not Alone* (New York: Harper, 1951), 59.

2. Ibid., 27.

3. Ibid., 11.

4. Ibid., 68.

5. *Gates of Prayer* (New York: Central Conference of American Rabbis, 1975), 157.

6. *Union Prayer Book*, Part I (New York: Central Conference of American Rabbis, 1961), 34.

Bibliography

Albo, J. *Book of Principles*. Edited by I. Husic. Philadelphia: Jewish Publication Society, 1946.

Anchor Bible Dictionary. New York: Doubleday, 1992.

Ancient Near Eastern Texts Relating to the Old Testament. 3d ed. Edited by James B. Pritchard. Princeton, N.J.: Princeton University, 1969.

Ariel, David S. *Spiritual Judaism*. New York: Hyperion, 1998.

Bernstein, Ellen, ed. *Ecology & the Jewish Spirit: Where Nature and the Sacred Meet*. Woodstock, Vt.: Jewish Lights, 1998.

Bialik, Hayim N., and Yehoshua H. Ravnitsky. *The Book of Legends*. Translated by William Braude. New York: Schocken, 1992.

Blank, Sheldon H. *Jeremiah*. Cincinnati: Hebrew Union College, 1961.

Blank, William. *Torah, Tarot and Tantra: A Guide to Jewish Spiritual Growth*. Boston: Coventure, 1991.

Boorstein, Sylvia. *That's Funny, You Don't Look Buddhist*. San Francisco: HarperSanFrancisco, 1996.

Buber, Martin. *Between Man and Man*. Translated by R. G. Smith. New York: Macmillan, 1965.

———. *I and Thou*. Translated by Walter Kaufmann. New York: Scribner's, 1970.

———. *Tales of the Hasidim: The Early Masters*. New York: Schocken, 1961.

———. *Tales of the Hasidim: The Later Masters*. New York: Schocken, 1948.

Chernick, Michael. "Spirituality and Danger." In *Paths of Faithfulness*, ed. Carol Ochs, Kerry M. Olitzky, and Joshua Saltzman. New York: KTAV, 1999: 17–25.

Childs, Brevard S. *The Book of Exodus. The Old Testament Library*. Philadelphia: Westminster Press, 1974.

Cohen, Martin A. "What Is Jewish Spirituality?" In *Paths of Faithfulness*, ed. Carol Ochs, Kerry M. Olitzky, and Joshua Saltzman. New York: KTAV, 1999: 27–34.

Cohen, Norman J. *The Way Into Torah*. Woodstock, Vt.: Jewish Lights, 2000.

Cooper, David A. *Three Gates to Meditation Practice: A Personal Journey into Sufism, Buddhism, and Judaism*. Woodstock, Vt.: SkyLight Paths, 2000. (Previous edition published as: *Entering the Sacred Mountain*. New York: Bell Tower, 1994.)

———. *God Is a Verb*. New York: Riverhead, 1997.

———. *The Handbook of Jewish Meditation Practices: A Guide for Enriching the Sabbath and Other Days of Your Life*. Woodstock, Vt.: Jewish Lights, 2000. (Previous edition published as: *Renewing Your Soul*. New York: Harper, 1995)

Davis, Avram. *The Way of Flame: A Guide to the Forgotten Mystical Tradition of Jewish Meditation*. Woodstock, Vt.: Jewish Lights, 1999.

Davis, Avram, ed. *Meditation from the Heart of Judaism: Today's Teachers Share Their Practices, Techniques, and Faith*. Woodstock, Vt.: Jewish Lights, 1999.

Dosick, Wayne. *Soul Judaism: Dancing with God into a New Era*. Woodstock, Vt.: Jewish Lights, 1999.

Essrig, Harry. "Sichat Chulin." *The American Rabbi* 24, no. 6. (June 1992): 2; cf. 27, no. 2. (Oct. 1994): 42.

Fine, Steven. "Did the Synagogue Replace the Temple?" *Biblical Review* (April 1996): 18–26, 41.

Firestone, Tirzah. *With Roots in Heaven*. New York: Dutton, 1998.

Fisdel, Steve. "Meditation as Our Own Jacob's Ladder." In *Meditation from the Heart of Judaism: Today's Teachers Share Their Practices, Techniques, and Faith*, ed. Avram Davis. Woodstock, Vt.: Jewish Lights, 1999: 121–130.

Frankiel, Tamar, and Judy Greenfeld. *Minding the Temple of the Soul: Balancing Body, Mind, and Spirit through Traditional Jewish Prayer, Movement, and Meditation*. Woodstock, Vt.: Jewish Lights, 1997.

Friedland, Eric F. "Shmuel Hugo Bergman: Philosopher and Believer." *Jewish Spectator* (Summer 1996): 32–34.

Fromm, Erich. *Psychoanalysis and Religion*. New Haven: Yale University Press, 1958.

———. *The Art of Loving*. New York: Harper, 1956.

Gates of Mitzvah. Edited by Simeon J. Maslin. New York: Central Conference of American Rabbis, 1979.

Gates of Prayer. New York: Central Conference of American Rabbis, 1975.

Gefen, Nan Fink. *Discovering Jewish Meditation: Instruction & Guidance for Learning an Ancient Spiritual Practice*. Woodstock, Vt.: Jewish Lights, 1999.

Gelfman, Harold "Letter to the Editor." *Central Conference of American Rabbis Newsletter* (May 1998).

Gillman, Neil. "Judaism and the Search for Spirituality." *Conservative Judaism* (Winter 1985/86): 5–18.

Gittelsohn, Roland B. "A Naturalist View." In *The Theological Foundations of Prayer*, ed. Jack Bemporad. New York: Union of American Hebrew Congregations, 1967: 43–52.

———. *Little Lower Than The Angels*. New York: Union of American Hebrew Congregations, 1955.

———. *Wings of the Morning*. New York: Union of American Hebrew Congregations, 1969.

Goldenberg, Robert. "Law and Spirit in the Talmudic Religion." In *Jewish Spirituality*, ed. by Arthur Green, New York: Crossroad, 1987: 232–252.

Goldin, Judah. *The Living Talmud*. New York: Signet, 1957.

Goldstein, Niles E. "The Spirituality of Shame." *Sh'ma* 28, no. 554 (May 15, 1998): 1–3.

Goldstein, Niles E., and Steven S. Mason. *Judaism and Spiritual Ethics*. New York: Union of American Hebrew Congregations, 1996.

Gray, John. *I and II Kings: A Commentary*. Philadelphia: Westminster Press, 1970: 406.

Green, Arthur. *Restoring the Aleph: Judaism for the Contemporary Seeker*. New York: Council for Initiatives in Jewish Education Series, 1996.

———. *These Are the Words: A Vocabulary of Jewish Spiritual Life*. Woodstock, Vt.: Jewish Lights, 1999.

Green, Arthur, ed. *Jewish Sprituality from the Bible through the Middle Ages*. New York: Crossroad, 1987.

Greenberg, Moshe. "On the Refinement of the Conception of Prayer in Hebrew Scriptures." *Association for Jewish Studies Review* 1, (1976): 57–92.

Hartman, David. *A Heart of Many Rooms: Celebrating the Many Voices within Judaism*. Woodstock, Vt.: Jewish Lights, 1999.

Heschel, Abraham Joshua. *Man Is Not Alone*. New York: Harper, 1951.

———. *Man's Quest for God*. New York: Scribner's, 1954.

Hoffman, Lawrence A. *My People's Prayer Book: Traditional Prayers, Modern Commentaries*, Vol. 3: *P'sukei D'zimrah*. Woodstock, Vt.: Jewish Lights, 1999.

———. *The Way to Jewish Prayer*. Woodstock, Vt.: Jewish Lights, 2000.

Hoffman, Lawrence A., and Arnold J. Wolf, eds. *Jewish Spiritual Journeys*. West Orange, N.J.: Behrman, 1997.

Jacobs, Louis. *Hasidic Thought*. West Orange, N.J.:Behrman, 1976.

———. *A Jewish Theology*. West Orange, N.J.: Behrman, 1973.

———. *The Book of Jewish Belief*. West Orange, N.J.: Behrman, 1984.

Kamenetz, Rodger. *The Jew in the Lotus*. San Francisco: Harper San Francisco, 1994.

Kaplan, Aryeh. *Jewish Meditation*. New York: Schocken, 1985.

Kaplan, Mordecai. *The Meaning of God in Modern Jewish Religion*. New York: Jewish Reconstructionist Press, 1962.

Katz, Robert L. *Empathy*. Glencoe, Ill.: Free Press, 1963.

Kedar, Karyn D. *God Whispers: Stories of the Soul, Lessons of the Heart*. Woodstock, Vt.: Jewish Lights, 1999.

Kertzer, Morris N. *What Is a Jew?* Revised by Lawrence A. Hoffman. New York: Macmillan, 1993.

Klagsbrun, Francine. "As Reform Turns Traditional." *Moment* (April 2000): 38–39.

———. "Feminine Spirituality." *Moment* (August 1992): 14–17.

Knobel, Peter S., ed. *The Gates of the Seasons*. New York: Central Conference of American Rabbis, 1983.

Kunin, Samuel. "Silent Prayer." *Berit Mila Newsletter* 4, no. 1 (May 25, 1992).

Kushner, Harold. *When Children Ask About God*. New York: Schocken, 1976.

———. *Who Needs God?* New York: Summit Books, 1989.

Kushner, Lawrence. "Facing the Unity of God." *Tikkun* (May/June 1992): 49–52, 94.

———. *Eyes Remade for Wonder: A Lawrence Kushner Reader*. Woodstock, Vt.: Jewish Lights, 1998.

———. *Invisible Lines of Connection: Sacred Stories of the Ordinary*. Woodstock, Vt.: Jewish Lights, 1996.

Labowitz, Shoni. "Prayer as Ecstasy and Art." In *Worlds of Jewish Prayer: A Festschrift in Honor of Rabbi Zalman M. Schachter-Shalomi*, ed. Jonathan Omer-Man. Northvale, N.J.: Jason Aronson, 1994: 47–50.

Lerner, Michael. *Jewish Renewal*. New York: Putnam, 1994.

Lew, Alan. "Prayer and the Uses of Meditation." *Judaism* (Winter 2000): 93–101.

———. "It Doesn't Matter What You Call It: If It Works, It Works." In *Meditation from the Heart of Judaism: Today's Teachers Share Their Practices, Techniques, and Faith*, ed. Avram Davis. Woodstock, Vt.: Jewish Lights, 1999: 43–52.

Liebman, Charles S. "When Prayer Becomes Leisure." *Forward* (June 11, 1999).

Lipman, Kennard. "On 'Meditation,' Jewish and Otherwise." *CCAR Journal* (Fall 1999): 21–27.

Maimonides, Moses. *Guide of the Perplexed*. Translated by S. Pines. Chicago: University of Chicago Press, 1963.

Matt, Daniel C. *God & the Big Bang: Discovering Harmony Between Science & Spirituality*. Woodstock, Vt.: Jewish Lights, 1996.

———. *The Essential Kabbalah*. Edison, N.J.: Castle Books, 1997.

McKibben, Bill. "JoysRUs." *Utne Reader* (March/April 2000): 60–64.

Mirel, James L., Karen Bonnell, and Werth. *Stepping Stones to Jewish Spiritual Living: Walking the Path Morning, Noon, and Night*. Woodstock, Vt.: Jewish Lights, 1998.

Montefiore, C. G., and H. Loewe. *A Rabbinic Anthology*. Philadelphia: Jewish Publication Society, 1962.

Moskowitz, Beth. "From the Temple President." Temple Aliyah, *Shofar*. Needham, Mass. (June 2000): 1, 8.

Moss, Steven, A. "Finding Spirituality through Meditation." *CCAR Journal* (Fall 1992): 47–52.

Neusner, Jacob. "Why I Am Not an Ethnic Jew, Why I Am a Religious Jew." *Jewish Spectator* (Winter 1996/7): 16–19.

Newman, Louis I. *Hasidic Anthology*. New York: Schocken, 1975.

Ochs, Carol, and Kerry M. Olitzky. *Jewish Spiritual Guidance*. San Francisco: Jossey-Bass, 1997.

Olitzky, Kerry M. "Towards a Personal Definition of Jewish Spirituality." In *Paths of Faithfulness*, ed. Carol Ochs, Kerry M. Olitzky, and Joshua Saltzman. New York: KTAV, 1999: 113–122.

Omer-Man, Jonathan. "Noble Boredom: How to View Meditation." In *Meditation from the Heart of Judaism: Today's Teachers Share Their Practices, Techniques, and Faith*, ed. Avram Davis. Woodstock, Vt.: Jewish Lights, 1999: 75–81.

Pines, Shlomo. *"Al ha-munah 'ruhaniyut' umeqorav ve'al mishnato shel Yehudah Halevi." Tarbitz* (July/September 1988): 511–540.

Plaut, Gunther W. *The Growth of Reform Judaism*. New York: World Union for Progressive Judaism, 1965.

———, ed. *The Torah—A Modern Commentary*. New York: Union of American Hebrew Congregations, 1981.

Portnoy, Mindy A. "Spirituality." *The American Rabbi* 27, no. 4 (February 1995): 17–24.

Prager, Marcia. *The Path of Blessing*. New York: Bell Tower, 1998.

Ribner, Mindy. "Keeping God Before Me Always." In *Meditation from the Heart of Judaism: Today's Teachers Share Their Practices, Techniques, and Faith*, ed. Avram Davis. Woodstock, Vt.: Jewish Lights, 1999: 63–73.

Ringgren, Helmer. *Israelite Religion*. Philadelphia: Fortress, 1963.

Sacks, Linda. "A God of Small Things." *Moment* (April 2000): 49.

Sagi, Avi. "Both Are the Words of the Living God." In *Hebrew Union College Annual*, Vol. 65. Cincinnati: HUCA, 1994: 105–136.

Saltzman, Joshua. "Talmud Torah and Spirituality." In *Paths of Faithfulness*, ed. Carol Ochs, Kerry M. Olitzky, and Joshua Saltzman. New York: KTAV, 1999: 137–156.

Sarna, Nahum. *The JPS Commentary—Genesis*. Philadelphia: Jewish Publication Society, 1989.

Scholem, Gershom. *Kabbalah*. New York: Meridian, 1978.

———. "Meditation." *Encyclopaedia Judaica*, Vol. 11, 1217ff.

———. *On the Kabbalah and Its Symbolism*. New York: Schocken, 1965.

Schulweis, Harold. "Between." In *Passages in Poetry*. Encino, Calif.: Valley Beth Shalom, 1990.

Sefer Hahinukh. Translated by Charles Wengrov. Jerusalem/New York: Feldheim, Vol. 5, 1992.

Shapiro, Deanne H. Jr., and Johanna Shapiro. "Spirituality in Reform Judaism." *Jewish Spectator* (Winter 1992): 31–33.

Shapiro, Rami M. *Minyan*. New York: Bell Tower, 1997.

Siegel, S., and E. Gertel, eds. *God in the Teachings of Conservative Judaism*. New York: Rabbinical Assembly, 1985.

Sonsino, Rifat. *Motive Clauses in Hebrew Law*. Dissertation Series 45. Chico, Calif.: SBL Scholars Press, 1980.

Sonsino, Rifat, and Daniel B. Syme. *Finding God*. New York: Union of American Hebrew Congregations, 1986.

Steinberg, Milton. *Basic Judaism*. New York: Harcourt, Brace and World, 1947.

Strassfeld, Michael. *The Jewish Holidays*. New York: Harper, 1985.

Telushkin, Joseph. *Jewish Literacy*. New York: William Morrow, 1991.

Tigay, Jeffrey H. *JPS Torah Commentary Deuteronomy*. Philadelphia: Jewish Publication Society, 1996.

Twersky, Isadore, ed. *A Maimonides Reader*. West Orange, N.J.: Behrman, 1972.

Union Prayer Book, Part I. New York: Central Conference of American Rabbis, 1961.

Urbach, E. E. *The Sages*. Cambridge, Mass.: Harvard University Press, 1979.

Vorspan, Albert. "The Jacques Attack." *Reform Judaism* (Spring 2000) 14–16.

Vorspan, Albert, and David Saperstein. *Tough Choices*. New York: Union of American Hebrew Congregations, 1992.

Waskow, Arthur. *Godwrestling—Round 2: Ancient Wisdom, Future Paths*. Woodstock, Vt.: Jewish Lights, 1996.

Weisblatt, Jeffrey J. "Spirituality." *The American Rabbi* (October 1993): 9–12.

Winkler, Gershon. "Davvening on a Prayer." In *Worlds of Jewish Prayer: A Festschrift in Honor of Rabbi Zalman M. Schachter-Shalomi*, ed. Jonathan Omer-Man. Northvale, N.J.: Jason Aronson, 1994: 17–21.

Winston, David. "Philo and the Contemplative Life." In *Jewish Spirituality*, ed. Arthur Green. New York: Crossroad, 1987: 198–231.

Winston, Diane. "Searching for Spirituality." *Moment* (June 1992): 28–35.

Wolfson, Ron. "My Top Ten Teaching Techniques." *Sh'ma* 24, no. 462 (November 26, 1993): 3–5.

Wolpe, David. *Teaching Your Children about God*. New York: Harper, 1995.

Yoffie, Eric H. "Remarks to the UAHC Executive Committee." New York: Union of American Hebrew Congregations, February 7, 2000: 1–3.

Zeller, David. "A Splendid Way to Live." In *Meditation from the Heart of Judaism: Today's Teachers Share Their Practices, Techniques, and Faith*, ed. Avram Davis. Woodstock, Vt.: Jewish Lights, 1999: 109–14.

Notes

Notes

Notes

About JEWISH LIGHTS Publishing

People of all faiths and backgrounds yearn for books that attract, engage, educate and spiritually inspire.

Our principal goal is to stimulate thought and help all people learn about who the Jewish People are, where they come from, and what the future can be made to hold. While people of our diverse Jewish heritage are the primary audience, our books speak to people in the Christian world as well and will broaden their understanding of Judaism and the roots of their own faith.

We bring to you authors who are at the forefront of spiritual thought and experience. While each has something different to say, they all say it in a voice that you can hear.

Our books are designed to welcome you and then to engage, stimulate and inspire. We judge our success not only by whether or not our books are beautiful and commercially successful, but by whether or not they make a difference in your life.

We at Jewish Lights take great care to produce beautiful books that present meaningful spiritual content in a form that reflects the art of making high quality books. Therefore, we want to acknowledge those who contributed to the production of this book.

Stuart M. Matlins, Publisher

PRODUCTION
Marian B. Wallace & Bridgett Taylor

EDITORIAL
Sandra Korinchak, Emily Wichland,
Martha McKinney & Amanda Dupuis

JACKET DESIGN
Kieran McCabe, Boston, Massachusetts

TEXT DESIGN
Terry Bain, Spokane, Washington

TYPESETTING
Jan Martí, Command Z, Palo Alto, California

JACKET & TEXT PRINTING AND BINDING
Lake Book, Melrose Park, Illinois

Life Cycle

Jewish Paths toward Healing and Wholeness
A Personal Guide to Dealing with Suffering
by *Rabbi Kerry M. Olitzky*; Foreword by *Debbie Friedman*

"Why me?" Why do we suffer? How can we heal? Grounded in the spiritual traditions of Judaism, this book provides healing rituals, psalms and prayers that help readers initiate a dialogue with God, to guide them along the complicated path of healing and wholeness. 6 x 9, 192 pp, Quality PB, ISBN 1-58023-068-7 **$15.95**

Mourning & Mitzvah: *A Guided Journal for Walking the Mourner's Path through Grief to Healing*
by *Anne Brener*, L.C.S.W.; Foreword by *Rabbi Jack Riemer*; Intro. by *Rabbi William Cutter*

For those who mourn a death, for those who would help them, for those who face a loss of any kind, Brener teaches us the power and strength available to us in the fully experienced mourning process. 7½ x 9, 288 pp, Quality PB, ISBN 1-879045-23-0 **$19.95**

Tears of Sorrow, Seeds of Hope
A Jewish Spiritual Companion for Infertility and Pregnancy Loss
by *Rabbi Nina Beth Cardin*

A spiritual companion that enables us to mourn infertility, a lost pregnancy, or a stillbirth within the prayers, rituals, and meditations of Judaism. By drawing on the texts of tradition, it creates readings and rites of mourning, and through them provides a wellspring of compassion, solace—and hope. 6 x 9, 192 pp, HC, ISBN 1-58023-017-2 **$19.95**

Lifecycles
V. 1: *Jewish Women on Life Passages & Personal Milestones* AWARD WINNER!
Ed. and with Intros. by Rabbi Debra Orenstein
V. 2: *Jewish Women on Biblical Themes in Contemporary Life* AWARD WINNER!
Ed. and with Intros. by Rabbi Debra Orenstein and Rabbi Jane Rachel Litman
V. 1: 6 x 9, 480 pp, Quality PB, ISBN 1-58023-018-0 **$19.95**; HC, ISBN 1-879045-14-1 **$24.95**
V. 2: 6 x 9, 464 pp, Quality PB, ISBN 1-58023-019-9 **$19.95**; HC, ISBN 1-879045-15-X **$24.95**

Grief in Our Seasons: *A Mourner's Kaddish Companion*
by Rabbi Kerry M. Olitzky 4½ x 6½, 448 pp, Quality PB, ISBN 1-879045-55-9 **$15.95**

A Time to Mourn, A Time to Comfort: *A Guide to Jewish Bereavement and Comfort*
by Dr. Ron Wolfson 7 x 9, 336 pp, Quality PB, ISBN 1-879045-96-6 **$16.95**

When a Grandparent Dies
A Kid's Own Remembering Workbook for Dealing with Shiva and the Year Beyond
by Nechama Liss-Levinson, Ph.D.
8 x 10, 48 pp, HC, Illus., 2-color text, ISBN 1-879045-44-3 **$15.95**

So That Your Values Live On: *Ethical Wills & How to Prepare Them*
Ed. by Rabbi Jack Riemer & Professor Nathaniel Stampfer
6 x 9, 272 pp, Quality PB, ISBN 1-879045-34-6 **$17.95**

Healing/Wellness/Recovery

Jewish Pastoral Care
A Practical Handbook from Traditional and Contemporary Sources
Ed. by *Rabbi Dayle A. Friedman*

This innovative resource builds on the classic foundations of pastoral care, enriching it with uniquely Jewish traditions and wisdom. Gives today's Jewish pastoral counselors practical guidelines based in the Jewish tradition. 6 x 9, 352 pp, HC, ISBN 1-58023-078-4 **$34.95** (Avail. Jan. 2001)

Healing of Soul, Healing of Body
Spiritual Leaders Unfold the Strength & Solace in Psalms
Ed. by *Rabbi Simkha Y. Weintraub*, CSW, for The National Center for Jewish Healing

A source of solace for those who are facing illness, as well as those who care for them. Provides a wellspring of strength with inspiring introductions and commentaries by eminent spiritual leaders reflecting all Jewish movements. 6 x 9, 128 pp, Quality PB, Illus., 2-color text, ISBN 1-879045-31-1 **$14.95**

Self, Struggle & Change: *Family Conflict Stories in Genesis and Their Healing Insights for Our Lives*
by *Dr. Norman J. Cohen*

How do I find wholeness in my life and in my family's life? Here a modern master of biblical interpretation brings us greater understanding of the ancient text and of ourselves in this intriguing re-telling of conflict between husband and wife, father and son, brothers and sisters. 6 x 9, 224 pp, Quality PB, ISBN 1-879045-66-4 **$16.95**; HC, ISBN 1-879045-19-2 **$21.95**

Twelve Jewish Steps to Recovery: *A Personal Guide to Turning from Alcoholism & Other Addictions . . . Drugs, Food, Gambling, Sex . . .* by Rabbi Kerry M. Olitzky & Stuart A. Copans, M.D. Preface by Abraham J. Twerski, M.D.; Intro. by Rabbi Sheldon Zimmerman; "Getting Help" by JACS Foundation 6 x 9, 144 pp, Quality PB, ISBN 1-879045-09-5 **$13.95**

One Hundred Blessings Every Day: *Daily Twelve Step Recovery Affirmations, Exercises for Personal Growth & Renewal Reflecting Seasons of the Jewish Year* by Rabbi Kerry M. Olitzky, with selected meditations prepared by Rabbi James Stone Goodman, Danny Siegel, and Gordon Tucker. Foreword by Rabbi Neil Gillman, The Jewish Theological Seminary of America; Afterword by Dr. Jay Holder, Director, Exodus Treatment Center 4½ x 6½, 432 pp, Quality PB, ISBN 1-879045-30-3 **$14.95**

Recovery from Codependence: *A Jewish Twelve Steps Guide to Healing Your Soul* by Rabbi Kerry M. Olitzky; Foreword by Marc Galanter, M.D., Director, Division of Alcoholism & Drug Abuse, NYU Medical Center; Afterword by Harriet Rossetto, Director, Gateways Beit T'shuvah 6 x 9, 160 pp, Quality PB, ISBN 1-879045-32-X **$13.95**; HC, ISBN 1-879045-27-3 **$21.95**

Renewed Each Day: *Daily Twelve Step Recovery Meditations Based on the Bible* by Rabbi Kerry M. Olitzky & Aaron Z. Vol. I: *Genesis & Exodus*; Intro. by Rabbi Michael A. Signer; Afterword by JACS Foundation. Vol. II: *Leviticus, Numbers and Deuteronomy*; Intro. by Sharon M. Strassfeld; Afterword by Rabbi Harold M. Schulweis
Vol. I: 6 x 9, 224 pp, Quality PB, ISBN 1-879045-12-5 **$14.95**
Vol. II: 6 x 9, 280 pp, Quality PB, ISBN 1-879045-13-3 **$14.95**

Theology/Philosophy

Torah of the Earth: *Exploring 4,000 Years of Ecology in Jewish Thought*
In 2 Volumes Ed. by *Rabbi Arthur Waskow*

Major new resource offering us an invaluable key to understanding the intersection of ecology and Judaism. Leading scholars provide us with a guided tour of ecological thought from four major Jewish viewpoints. Vol. 1: *Biblical Israel & Rabbinic Judaism,* 6 x 9, 272 pp, Quality PB, ISBN 1-58023-086-5 **$19.95**; Vol. 2: *Zionism & Eco-Judaism,* 6 x 9, 336 pp, Quality PB, ISBN 1-58023-087-3 **$19.95**

Broken Tablets: *Restoring the Ten Commandments and Ourselves*
Ed. by *Rabbi Rachel S. Mikva*; Intro. by *Rabbi Lawrence Kushner*;
Afterword by *Rabbi Arnold Jacob Wolf* **AWARD WINNER!**

Twelve outstanding spiritual leaders each share profound and personal thoughts about these biblical commands and why they have such a special hold on us.
6 x 9, 192 pp, HC, ISBN 1-58023-066-0 **$21.95**

Evolving Halakhah: *A Progressive Approach to Traditional Jewish Law*
by *Rabbi Dr. Moshe Zemer*

Innovative and provocative, this book affirms the system of traditional Jewish law, *halakhah,* as flexible enough to accommodate the changing realities of each generation. It shows that the traditional framework for understanding the Torah's commandments can be the living heart of Jewish life for all Jews. 6 x 9, 480 pp, HC, ISBN 1-58023-002-4 **$40.00**

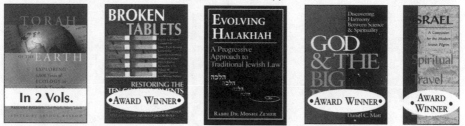

God & the Big Bang
Discovering Harmony Between Science & Spirituality **AWARD WINNER!**
by Daniel C. Matt
6 x 9, 216 pp, Quality PB, ISBN 1-879045-89-3 **$16.95**; HC, ISBN 1-879045-48-6 **$21.95**

Israel—A Spiritual Travel Guide **AWARD WINNER!**
A Companion for the Modern Jewish Pilgrim
by Rabbi Lawrence A. Hoffman 4¾ x 10, 256 pp, Quality PB, ISBN 1-879045-56-7 **$18.95**

Godwrestling—Round 2: *Ancient Wisdom, Future Paths* **AWARD WINNER!**
by Rabbi Arthur Waskow
6 x 9, 352 pp, Quality PB, ISBN 1-879045-72-9 **$18.95**; HC, ISBN 1-879045-45-1 **$23.95**

Ecology & the Jewish Spirit: *Where Nature & the Sacred Meet* Ed. and with Intros. by
Ellen Bernstein 6 x 9, 288 pp, Quality PB, ISBN 1-58023-082-2 **$16.95**;
HC, ISBN 1-879045-88-5 **$23.95**

Israel: *An Echo of Eternity* by Abraham Joshua Heschel; New Intro. by
Dr. Susannah Heschel 5½ x 8, 272 pp, Quality PB, ISBN 1-879045-70-2 **$18.95**

The Earth Is the Lord's: *The Inner World of the Jew in Eastern Europe*
by Abraham Joshua Heschel 5½ x 8, 112 pp, Quality PB, ISBN 1-879045-42-7 **$13.95**

A Passion for Truth: *Despair and Hope in Hasidism* by Abraham Joshua Heschel
5½ x 8, 352 pp, Quality PB, ISBN 1-879045-41-9 **$18.95**

Theology/Philosophy

A Heart of Many Rooms
Celebrating the Many Voices within Judaism
by *Dr. David Hartman* AWARD WINNER!

Named a *Publishers Weekly* "Best Book of the Year." Addresses the spiritual and theological questions that face all Jews and all people today. From the perspective of traditional Judaism, Hartman shows that commitment to both Jewish tradition and to pluralism can create understanding between people of different religious convictions.
6 x 9, 352 pp, HC, ISBN 1-58023-048-2 **$24.95**

A Living Covenant: *The Innovative Spirit in Traditional Judaism*
by *Dr. David Hartman* AWARD WINNER!

Winner, National Jewish Book Award. Hartman reveals a Judaism grounded in covenant—a relational framework—informed by the metaphor of marital love rather than that of parent-child dependency. 6 x 9, 368 pp, Quality PB, ISBN 1-58023-011-3 **$18.95**

The Death of Death: *Resurrection and Immortality in Jewish Thought*
by *Dr. Neil Gillman* AWARD WINNER!

Does death end life, or is it the passage from one stage of life to another? This National Jewish Book Award Finalist explores the original and compelling argument that Judaism, a religion often thought to pay little attention to the afterlife, not only offers us rich ideas on the subject—but delivers a deathblow to death itself. 6 x 9, 336 pp, Quality PB, ISBN 1-58023-081-4 **$18.95**; HC, ISBN 1-879045-61-3 **$23.95**

Aspects of Rabbinic Theology by Solomon Schechter; New Intro. by Dr. Neil Gillman
6 x 9, 448 pp, Quality PB, ISBN 1-879045-24-9 **$19.95**

The Last Trial: *On the Legends and Lore of the Command to Abraham to Offer Isaac as a Sacrifice* by Shalom Spiegel; New Intro. by Judah Goldin
6 x 9, 208 pp, Quality PB, ISBN 1-879045-29-X **$17.95**

Judaism and Modern Man: *An Interpretation of Jewish Religion* by Will Herberg;
New Intro. by Dr. Neil Gillman 5½ x 8½, 336 pp, Quality PB, ISBN 1-879045-87-7 **$18.95**

Seeking the Path to Life AWARD WINNER!
Theological Meditations on God and the Nature of People, Love, Life and Death
by Rabbi Ira F. Stone
6 x 9, 160 pp, Quality PB, ISBN 1-879045-47-8 **$14.95**; HC, ISBN 1-879045-17-6 **$19.95**

The Spirit of Renewal: *Finding Faith after the Holocaust* AWARD WINNER!
by Rabbi Edward Feld
6 x 9, 224 pp, Quality PB, ISBN 1-879045-40-0 **$16.95**

Tormented Master: *The Life and Spiritual Quest of Rabbi Nahman of Bratslav*
by Dr. Arthur Green
6 x 9, 416 pp, Quality PB, ISBN 1-879045-11-7 **$18.95**

Your Word Is Fire: *The Hasidic Masters on Contemplative Prayer*
Ed. and Trans. with a New Introduction by Dr. Arthur Green and Dr. Barry W. Holtz
6 x 9, 160 pp, Quality PB, ISBN 1-879045-25-7 **$14.95**

Life Cycle & Holidays

How to Be a Perfect Stranger, In 2 Volumes
A Guide to Etiquette in Other People's Religious Ceremonies
Ed. by *Stuart M. Matlins* & *Arthur J. Magida* AWARD WINNER!

What will happen? What do I do? What do I wear? What do I say? What should I avoid doing, wearing, saying? What are their basic beliefs? Should I bring a gift? In question-and-answer format, *How to Be a Perfect Stranger* explains the rituals and celebrations of America's major religions/denominations, helping an interested guest to feel comfortable, participate to the fullest extent possible, and avoid violating anyone's religious principles. It is not a guide to theology, nor is it presented from the perspective of any particular faith.

Vol. 1: *America's Largest Faiths*, 6 x 9, 432 pp, HC, ISBN 1-879045-39-7 **$24.95**
Vol. 2: *Other Faiths in America*, 6 x 9, 416 pp, HC, ISBN 1-879045-63-X **$24.95**

Putting God on the Guest List, 2nd Ed.
How to Reclaim the Spiritual Meaning of Your Child's Bar or Bat Mitzvah
by *Rabbi Jeffrey K. Salkin* AWARD WINNER!

The expanded, updated, revised edition of today's most influential book (over 60,000 copies in print) about finding core spiritual values in American Jewry's most misunderstood ceremony.
6 x 9, 224 pp, Quality PB, ISBN 1-879045-59-1 **$16.95**; HC, ISBN 1-879045-58-3 **$24.95**

For Kids—Putting God on Your Guest List
How to Claim the Spiritual Meaning of Your Bar or Bat Mitzvah
by Rabbi Jeffrey K. Salkin 6 x 9, 144 pp, Quality PB, ISBN 1-58023-015-6 **$14.95**

Bar/Bat Mitzvah Basics
A Practical Family Guide to Coming of Age Together
Ed. by Cantor Helen Leneman 6 x 9, 240 pp, Quality PB, ISBN 1-879045-54-0 **$16.95**; HC, ISBN 1-879045-51-6 **$24.95**

The New Jewish Baby Book AWARD WINNER!
Names, Ceremonies, & Customs—A Guide for Today's Families
by Anita Diamant 6 x 9, 336 pp, Quality PB, ISBN 1-879045-28-1 **$16.95**

Hanukkah: The Art of Jewish Living
by Dr. Ron Wolfson 7 x 9, 192 pp, Quality PB, Illus., ISBN 1-879045-97-4 **$16.95**

The Shabbat Seder: The Art of Jewish Living
by Dr. Ron Wolfson 7 x 9, 272 pp, Quality PB, Illus., ISBN 1-879045-90-7 **$16.95**
Also available are these helpful companions to *The Shabbat Seder*: Booklet of the Blessings and Songs, ISBN 1-879045-91-5 **$5.00**; Audiocassette of the Blessings, DN03 **$6.00**; Teacher's Guide, ISBN 1-879045-92-3 **$4.95**

The Passover Seder: The Art of Jewish Living
by Dr. Ron Wolfson 7 x 9, 352 pp, Quality PB, Illus., ISBN 1-879045-93-1 **$16.95**
Also available are these helpful companions to *The Passover Seder*: Passover Workbook, ISBN 1-879045-94-X **$6.95**; Audiocassette of the Blessings, DN04 **$6.00**; Teacher's Guide, ISBN 1-879045-95-8 **$4.95**

Children's Spirituality

God Said Amen
by *Sandy Eisenberg Sasso*
Full-color illus. by *Avi Katz*

For ages
4 & up

MULTICULTURAL, NONDENOMINATIONAL, NONSECTARIAN

A warm and inspiring tale of two kingdoms: Midnight Kingdom is overflowing with water but has no oil to light its lamps; Desert Kingdom is blessed with oil but has no water to grow its gardens. The kingdoms' rulers ask God for help but are too stubborn to ask each other. It takes a minstrel, a pair of royal riding-birds and their young keepers, and a simple act of kindness to show that they need only reach out to each other to find God's answer to their prayers.

9 x 12, 32 pp, HC, Full-color illus., ISBN 1-58023-080-6 **$16.95**

For Heaven's Sake
by *Sandy Eisenberg Sasso*; Full-color illus. by *Kathryn Kunz Finney*

For ages
4 & up

MULTICULTURAL, NONDENOMINATIONAL, NONSECTARIAN

Everyone talked about heaven: "Thank heavens." "Heaven forbid." "For heaven's sake, Isaiah." But no one would say what heaven was or how to find it. So Isaiah decides to find out, by seeking answers from many different people. "This book is a reminder of how well Sandy Sasso knows the minds of children. But it may surprise—and delight—readers to find how well she knows us grown-ups too." —*Maria Harris*, National Consultant in Religious Education, and author of *Teaching and Religious Imagination* 9 x 12, 32 pp, HC, Full-color illus., ISBN 1-58023-054-7 **$16.95**

But God Remembered: Stories of Women from Creation to the Promised Land
by *Sandy Eisenberg Sasso*; Full-color illus. by *Bethanne Andersen*

For ages
8 & up

NONDENOMINATIONAL, NONSECTARIAN

A fascinating collection of four different stories of women only briefly mentioned in biblical tradition and religious texts. Award-winning author Sasso vibrantly brings to life courageous and strong women from ancient tradition; all teach important values through their actions and faith. "Exquisite. . . . A book of beauty, strength and spirituality." —*Association of Bible Teachers* 9 x 12, 32 pp, HC, Full-color illus., ISBN 1-879045-43-5 **$16.95**

God in Between
by *Sandy Eisenberg Sasso*; Full-color illus. by *Sally Sweetland*

For ages
4 & up

MULTICULTURAL, NONDENOMINATIONAL, NONSECTARIAN

If you wanted to find God, where would you look? A magical, mythical tale that teaches that God can be found where we are: within all of us and the relationships between us. "This happy and wondrous book takes our children on a sweet and holy journey into God's presence." —*Rabbi Wayne Dosick*, Ph.D., author of *Golden Rules* and *Soul Judaism*
9 x 12, 32 pp, HC, Full-color illus., ISBN 1-879045-86-9 **$16.95**

Children's Spirituality

In Our Image
God's First Creatures
by *Nancy Sohn Swartz*
Full-color illus. by *Melanie Hall*

For ages
4 & up

NONDENOMINATIONAL, NONSECTARIAN

A playful new twist on the Creation story—from the perspective of the animals. Celebrates the interconnectedness of nature and the harmony of all living things. "The vibrantly colored illustrations nearly leap off the page in this delightful interpretation." —*School Library Journal*

"A message all children should hear, presented in words and pictures that children will find irresistible." —*Rabbi Harold Kushner,* author of *When Bad Things Happen to Good People*

9 x 12, 32 pp, HC, Full-color illus., ISBN 1-879045-99-0 **$16.95**

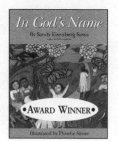

God's Paintbrush
by *Sandy Eisenberg Sasso*; Full-color illus. by *Annette Compton*

For ages
4 & up

MULTICULTURAL, NONDENOMINATIONAL, NONSECTARIAN

Invites children of all faiths and backgrounds to encounter God openly in their own lives. Wonderfully interactive; provides questions adult and child can explore together at the end of each episode. "An excellent way to honor the imaginative breadth and depth of the spiritual life of the young." —*Dr. Robert Coles,* Harvard University
11 x 8½, 32 pp, HC, Full-color illus., ISBN 1-879045-22-2 **$16.95**

Also available: A Teacher's Guide: **A Guide for Jewish & Christian Educators and Parents**
8½ x 11, 32 pp, PB, ISBN 1-879045-57-5 **$6.95**

God's Paintbrush Celebration Kit 9½ x 12, HC, Includes 5 sessions/40 full-color Activity Sheets and Teacher Folder with complete instructions, ISBN 1-58023-050-4 **$21.95**

In God's Name
by *Sandy Eisenberg Sasso*; Full-color illus. by *Phoebe Stone*

For ages
4 & up

MULTICULTURAL, NONDENOMINATIONAL, NONSECTARIAN

Like an ancient myth in its poetic text and vibrant illustrations, this award-winning modern fable about the search for God's name celebrates the diversity and, at the same time, the unity of all the people of the world. "What a lovely, healing book!" —*Madeleine L'Engle*
9 x 12, 32 pp, HC, Full-color illus., ISBN 1-879045-26-5 **$16.95**

What Is God's Name? (A Board Book)
An abridged board book version of the award-winning *In God's Name.*
5 x 5, 24 pp, Board, Full-color illus., ISBN 1-893361-10-1 **$7.95**

For ages
0–4

Children's Spirituality

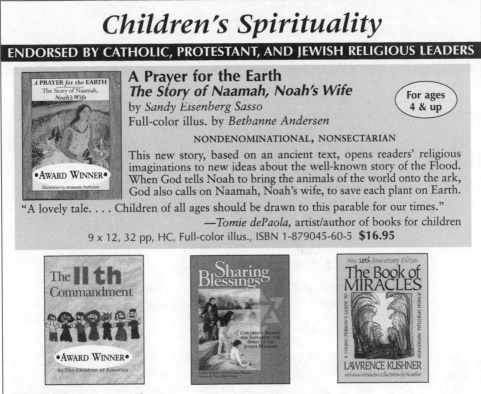

A Prayer for the Earth
The Story of Naamah, Noah's Wife
by *Sandy Eisenberg Sasso*
Full-color illus. by *Bethanne Andersen*

For ages 4 & up

NONDENOMINATIONAL, NONSECTARIAN

This new story, based on an ancient text, opens readers' religious imaginations to new ideas about the well-known story of the Flood. When God tells Noah to bring the animals of the world onto the ark, God also calls on Naamah, Noah's wife, to save each plant on Earth.

"A lovely tale. . . . Children of all ages should be drawn to this parable for our times."
—*Tomie dePaola*, artist/author of books for children

9 x 12, 32 pp, HC, Full-color illus., ISBN 1-879045-60-5 **$16.95**

The 11th Commandment: Wisdom from Our Children
by *The Children of America*

For all ages

MULTICULTURAL, NONDENOMINATIONAL, NONSECTARIAN

"If there were an Eleventh Commandment, what would it be?" Children of many religious denominations across America answer this question—in their own drawings and words. "A rare book of spiritual celebration for all people, of all ages, for all time."—*Bookviews*
8 x 10, 48 pp, HC, Full-color illus., ISBN 1-879045-46-X **$16.95**

Sharing Blessings: Children's Stories for Exploring the Spirit of the Jewish Holidays
by *Rahel Musleah* and *Rabbi Michael Klayman*
Full-color illus. by *Mary O'Keefe Young*

For ages 6 & up

What is the spiritual message of each of the Jewish holidays? How do we teach it to our children? Many books tell children about the historical significance and customs of the holidays. Now, through engaging, creative stories about one family's preparation, *Sharing Blessings* explores ways to get into the *spirit* of 13 different holidays. "Lighthearted, and yet thorough—allows all Jewish parents (even those with very little Jewish education) to introduce the spirit of our cherished holiday traditions." —*Shari Lewis*, creator and star of PBS' *Lamb Chop's Play-Along*
8½ x 11, 64 pp, HC, Full-color illus., ISBN 1-879045-71-0 **$18.95**

The Book of Miracles
A Young Person's Guide to Jewish Spiritual Awareness
by *Lawrence Kushner*

For ages 9 & up

From the miracle at the Red Sea to the miracle of waking up this morning, this intriguing book introduces kids to a way of everyday spiritual thinking to last a lifetime. Kushner, whose award-winning books have brought spirituality to life for countless adults, now shows young people how to use Judaism as a foundation on which to build their lives. "A well-written, easy to understand, very lovely guide to Jewish spirituality. I recommend it to all teens as a good read." —*Kimberly Kirberger*, co-author, *Chicken Soup for the Teenage Soul* 6 x 9, 96 pp, HC, 2-color illus., ISBN 1-879045-78-8 **$16.95**

Spirituality & More

These Are the Words: *A Vocabulary of Jewish Spiritual Life*
by *Arthur Green*

What are the most essential ideas, concepts and terms that an educated person needs to know about Judaism? From *Adonai* (My Lord) to *zekhut* (merit), this enlightening and entertaining journey through Judaism teaches us the 149 core Hebrew words that constitute the basic vocabulary of Jewish spiritual life. 6 x 9, 304 pp, HC, ISBN 1-58023-024-5 **$21.95**

The Enneagram and Kabbalah: *Reading Your Soul*
by *Rabbi Howard A. Addison*

Combines two of the most powerful maps of consciousness known to humanity—The Tree of Life (the *Sefirot*) from the Jewish mystical tradition of *Kabbalah*, and the nine-pointed Enneagram—and shows how, together, they can provide a powerful tool for self-knowledge, critique, and transformation. 6 x 9, 176 pp, Quality PB, ISBN 1-58023-001-6 **$15.95**

Embracing the Covenant
Converts to Judaism Talk About Why & How
Ed. and with Intros. by *Rabbi Allan L. Berkowitz* and *Patti Moskovitz*

Through personal experiences of 20 converts to Judaism, this book illuminates reasons for converting, the quest for a satisfying spirituality, the appeal of the Jewish tradition and how conversion has changed lives—the convert's, and the lives of those close to them. 6 x 9, 192 pp, Quality PB, ISBN 1-879045-50-8 **$15.95**

Shared Dreams: *Martin Luther King, Jr. and the Jewish Community*
by Rabbi Marc Schneier; Preface by Martin Luther King III
6 x 9, 240 pp, HC, ISBN 1-58023-062-8 **$24.95**

Mystery Midrash: *An Anthology of Jewish Mystery & Detective Fiction*
Ed. by Lawrence W. Raphael; Preface by Joel Siegel, ABC's *Good Morning America*
6 x 9, 304 pp, Quality PB, ISBN 1-58023-055-5 **$16.95**

The Jewish Gardening Cookbook: *Growing Plants & Cooking for Holidays & Festivals*
by Michael Brown 6 x 9, 224 pp, HC, Illus., ISBN 1-58023-004-0 **$21.95**

Wandering Stars: *An Anthology of Jewish Fantasy & Science Fiction* Ed. by Jack Dann; Intro. by Isaac Asimov 6 x 9, 272 pp, Quality PB, ISBN 1-58023-005-9 **$16.95**

More Wandering Stars
An Anthology of Outstanding Stories of Jewish Fantasy and Science Fiction
Ed. by Jack Dann; Intro. by Isaac Asimov 6 x 9, 192 pp, Quality PB, ISBN 1-58023-063-6 **$16.95**

A Heart of Wisdom: *Making the Jewish Journey from Midlife through the Elder Years*
Ed. by Susan Berrin; Foreword by Harold Kushner
6 x 9, 384 pp, Quality PB, ISBN 1-58023-051-2 **$18.95**; HC, ISBN 1-879045-73-7 **$24.95**

Sacred Intentions: *Daily Inspiration to Strengthen the Spirit, Based on Jewish Wisdom*
by Rabbi Kerry M. Olitzky and Rabbi Lori Forman
4½ x 6½, 448 pp, Quality PB, ISBN 1-58023-061-X **$15.95**

Jewish Meditation

Discovering Jewish Meditation
Instruction & Guidance for Learning an Ancient Spiritual Practice
by *Nan Fink Gefen*

Gives readers of any level of understanding the tools to learn the practice of Jewish meditation on your own, starting you on the path to a deep spiritual and personal connection to God and to greater insight about your life. 6 x 9, 208 pp, Quality PB, ISBN 1-58023-067-9 **$16.95**

Meditation from the Heart of Judaism: *Today's Teachers Share Their Practices, Techniques, and Faith*
Ed. by *Avram Davis*

A "how-to"guide for both beginning and experienced meditators, drawing on the wisdom of 22 masters of meditation who explain why and how they meditate. A detailed compendium of the experts' "best practices" offers advice and starting points. 6 x 9, 256 pp, Quality PB, ISBN 1-58023-049-0 **$16.95**; HC, ISBN 1-879045-77-X **$21.95**

The Way of Flame
A Guide to the Forgotten Mystical Tradition of Jewish Meditation
by *Avram Davis* 4½ x 8, 176 pp, Quality PB, ISBN 1-58023-060-1 **$15.95**

Entering the Temple of Dreams: *Jewish Prayers, Movements, and Meditations for the End of the Day* by *Tamar Frankiel* and *Judy Greenfeld*
Nighttime spirituality is much more than bedtime prayers! Here, you'll uncover deeper meaning to familiar nighttime prayers—and learn to combine the prayers with movements and meditations to enhance your physical and psychological well-being.
7 x 10, 192 pp, Illus., Quality PB, ISBN 1-58023-079-2 **$16.95**

Minding the Temple of the Soul: *Balancing Body, Mind, and Spirit through Traditional Jewish Prayer, Movement, and Meditation*
by *Tamar Frankiel* and *Judy Greenfeld*

This new spiritual approach to physical health introduces readers to a spiritual tradition that affirms the body and enables them to reconceive their bodies in a more positive light. Focuses on traditional Jewish prayers, with exercises, movements, and meditations. 7 x 10, 184 pp, Quality PB, Illus., ISBN 1-879045-64-8 **$16.95**; Audiotape of the Blessings, Movements and Meditations (60-min. cassette), JN01 **$9.95**; Videotape of the Movements and Meditations (46-min. VHS), S507 **$20.00**

Spirituality—The Kushner Series

Honey from the Rock, Special Anniversary Edition
An Introduction to Jewish Mysticism
by *Lawrence Kushner*

An insightful and absorbing introduction to the ten gates of Jewish mysticism and how it applies to daily life. "The easiest introduction to Jewish mysticism you can read."
6 x 9, 176 pp, Quality PB, ISBN 1-58023-073-3 **$15.95**

Eyes Remade for Wonder
The Way of Jewish Mysticism and Sacred Living
A Lawrence Kushner Reader

Intro. by *Thomas Moore*

Whether you are new to Kushner or a devoted fan, you'll find inspiration here. With samplings from each of Kushner's works, and a generous amount of new material, this book is to be read and reread, each time discovering deeper layers of meaning in our lives.
6 x 9, 240 pp, Quality PB, ISBN 1-58023-042-3 **$16.95**; HC, ISBN 1-58023-014-8 **$23.95**

Invisible Lines of Connection
Sacred Stories of the Ordinary
by *Lawrence Kushner* AWARD WINNER!

Through his everyday encounters with family, friends, colleagues and strangers, Kushner takes us deeply into our lives, finding flashes of spiritual insight in the process.
6 x 9, 160 pp, Quality PB, ISBN 1-879045-98-2 **$15.95**; HC, ISBN 1-879045-52-4 **$21.95**

The Book of Letters
A Mystical Hebrew Alphabet AWARD WINNER!
by Lawrence Kushner

Popular HC Edition, 6 x 9, 80 pp, 2-color text, ISBN 1-879045-00-1 **$24.95**; *Deluxe Gift Edition*, 9 x 12, 80 pp, HC, 2-color text, ornamentation, slipcase, ISBN 1-879045-01-X **$79.95**; *Collector's Limited Edition*, 9 x 12, 80 pp, HC, gold-embossed pages, hand-assembled slipcase. With silkscreened print. Limited to 500 signed and numbered copies, ISBN 1-879045-04-4 **$349.00**

The Book of Words
Talking Spiritual Life, Living Spiritual Talk AWARD WINNER!
by Lawrence Kushner 6 x 9, 160 pp, Quality PB, 2-color text, ISBN 1-58023-020-2 **$16.95**; 152 pp, HC, ISBN 1-879045-35-4 **$21.95**

God Was in This Place & I, i Did Not Know
Finding Self, Spirituality & Ultimate Meaning
by Lawrence Kushner 6 x 9, 192 pp, Quality PB, ISBN 1-879045-33-8 **$16.95**

The River of Light: *Jewish Mystical Awareness*
by Lawrence Kushner 6 x 9, 192 pp, Quality PB, ISBN 1-879045-03-6 **$14.95**

Spirituality

My People's Prayer Book: *Traditional Prayers, Modern Commentaries*
Ed. by *Dr. Lawrence A. Hoffman*
This momentous, critically-acclaimed series is truly a people's prayer book, one that provides a diverse and exciting commentary to the traditional liturgy. It will help modern men and women find new wisdom and guidance in Jewish prayer, and bring liturgy into their lives. Each book includes Hebrew text, modern translation, and commentaries *from all perspectives* of the Jewish world. Vol. 1—*The Sh'ma and Its Blessings,* 7 x 10, 168 pp, HC, ISBN 1-879045-79-6 **$23.95**
Vol. 2—*The Amidah,* 7 x 10, 240 pp, HC, ISBN 1-879045-80-X **$23.95**
Vol. 3—*P'sukei D'zimrah* (Morning Psalms), 7 x 10, 240 pp, HC, ISBN 1-879045-81-8 **$23.95**
Vol. 4—*Seder K'riyat Hatorah* (Shabbat Torah Service), 7 x 10, 240 pp, ISBN 1-879045-82-6 **$23.95**
(Avail. Nov. 2000)

Voices from Genesis: *Guiding Us through the Stages of Life*
by *Dr. Norman J. Cohen*
In a brilliant blending of modern *midrash* (finding contemporary meaning from biblical texts) and the life stages of Erik Erikson's developmental psychology, the characters of Genesis come alive to give us insights for our own journeys. 6 x 9, 192 pp, HC, ISBN 1-879045-75-3 **$21.95**

God Whispers: *Stories of the Soul, Lessons of the Heart*
by Rabbi Karyn D. Kedar 6 x 9, 176 pp, Quality PB, ISBN 1-58023-088-1 **$15.95**;
HC, ISBN 1-58023-023-7 **$19.95**

Being God's Partner: *How to Find the Hidden Link Between Spirituality and Your Work*
by Rabbi Jeffrey K. Salkin; Intro. by Norman Lear AWARD WINNER!
6 x 9, 192 pp, Quality PB, ISBN 1-879045-65-6 **$16.95**; HC, ISBN 1-879045-37-0 **$19.95**

ReVisions: *Seeing Torah through a Feminist Lens* AWARD WINNER!
by Rabbi Elyse Goldstein 5½ x 8½, 208 pp, HC, ISBN 1-58023-047-4 **$19.95**

Soul Judaism: *Dancing with God into a New Era*
by Rabbi Wayne Dosick 5½ x 8½, 304 pp, Quality PB, ISBN 1-58023-053-9 **$16.95**

Finding Joy: *A Practical Spiritual Guide to Happiness* AWARD WINNER!
by Rabbi Dannel I. Schwartz with Mark Hass
6 x 9, 192 pp, Quality PB, ISBN 1-58023-009-1 **$14.95**; HC, ISBN 1-879045-53-2 **$19.95**

The Empty Chair: *Finding Hope and Joy—*
Timeless Wisdom from a Hasidic Master, Rebbe Nachman of Breslov AWARD WINNER!
Adapted by Moshe Mykoff and the Breslov Research Institute
4 x 6, 128 pp, Deluxe PB, 2-color text, ISBN 1-879045-67-2 **$9.95**

The Gentle Weapon: *Prayers for Everyday and Not-So-Everyday Moments*
Adapted from the Wisdom of Rebbe Nachman of Breslov by Moshe Mykoff and
S. C. Mizrahi, with the Breslov Research Institute
4 x 6, 144 pp, Deluxe PB, 2-color text, ISBN 1-58023-022-9 **$9.95**

"Who Is a Jew?" *Conversations, Not Conclusions* by Meryl Hyman
6 x 9, 272 pp, Quality PB, ISBN 1-58023-052-0 **$16.95**; HC, ISBN 1-879045-76-1 **$23.95**

Spirituality

The Women's Torah Commentary: New Insights from Women Rabbis on the 54 Weekly Torah Portions Ed. by Rabbi Elyse Goldstein

For the first time, women rabbis provide a commentary on the entire Torah. More than 25 years after the first woman was ordained a rabbi in America, women have an impressive group of spiritual role models that they never had before. Here, in a week-by-week format, these inspiring teachers bring their rich perspectives to bear on the biblical text. A perfect gift for others, or for yourself. 6 x 9, 496 pp, HC, ISBN 1-58023-076-8 **$34.95**

Bringing the Psalms to Life
How to Understand and Use the Book of Psalms by Rabbi Daniel F. Polish

Here, the most beloved—and least understood—of the books in the Bible comes alive. This simultaneously insightful and practical guide shows how the psalms address a myriad of spiritual issues in our lives: feeling abandoned, overcoming illness, dealing with anger, and more. 6 x 9, 208 pp, HC, ISBN 1-58023-077-6 **$21.95**

Stepping Stones to Jewish Spiritual Living: Walking the Path
Morning, Noon, and Night by Rabbi James L. Mirel & Karen Bonnell Werth

Transforms our daily routine into sacred acts of mindfulness. Chapters are arranged according to the cycle of each day. "A wonderful, practical, and inspiring guidebook to gently bring the riches of Jewish practice into our busy, everyday lives. Highly recommended." —*Rabbi David A. Cooper.* 6 x 9, 240 pp, Quality PB, ISBN 1-58023-074-1 **$16.95**; HC, ISBN 1-58023-003-2 **$21.95**

Parenting As a Spiritual Journey:
Deepening Ordinary & Extraordinary Events into Sacred Occasions
by Rabbi Nancy Fuchs-Kreimer 6 x 9, 224 pp, Quality PB, ISBN 1-58023-016-4 **$16.95**

The Year Mom Got Religion: *One Woman's Midlife Journey into Judaism*
by Lee Meyerhoff Hendler 6 x 9, 208 pp, Quality PB, ISBN 1-58023-070-9 **$15.95**; HC, ISBN 1-58023-000-8 **$19.95**

Moses—The Prince, the Prophet: *His Life, Legend & Message for Our Lives*
by Rabbi Levi Meier, Ph.D. 6 x 9, 224 pp, Quality PB, ISBN 1-58023-069-5 **$16.95**; HC, ISBN 1-58023-013-X **$23.95**

Ancient Secrets: *Using the Stories of the Bible to Improve Our Everyday Lives*
by Rabbi Levi Meier, Ph.D. 5½ x 8½, 288 pp, Quality PB, ISBN 1-58023-064-4 **$16.95**